T: Reloaded

Contains: T: Ghosts in the Machine ISBN 978-0-9908570-7-5

Published by DiaryUnlimited, an imprint of The Edge Press.

AnotherClip.com

Table of Contents

Page numbers may differ.

Prologue

Situation

This is supposed to be read as a novel; albeit perhaps an agonising series of events, but not a pamphlet of facts and figures with endless references and evidence of all kinds.

The world consists of two dimensions: The Positive and the Negative. The Negative dimension is like an unprocessed side of what used to be a photographic picture: this is dark matter. The Positive is the world in full colour where I'm supposed to live. In reality we're not. We live in the Negative. We never die there. Thousands of years of living creatures are all living in the Negative dimension. It's never ending whereas in the Positive dimension, we only have one life.

The world in the Positive dimension is merely an optical illusion created by aliens and extra-terrestrial forces and is all part of a virtual game. The Negative dimension is where the creatures from the Positive dimension go to when they have failed their game. It is a rarity when one creature succeeds in crossing the different dimensions back and forth. This means they have overpowered the forces from above and this can trigger very complex energies. The Positive dimension is pure entertainment for the aliens above and in turn for the creatures from the Positive dimension to be entertained.

Chapter One: G and Me.

It's really tough to survive in London especially if you start at the bottom end. No one cares if you're in the gutter; you're always all alone in this world. Most people would think you deserve it. You are either born one way or another: rich or poor. People who are poor remain poor and people who are rich remain rich and neither the twain shall meet. Except that this popular concept is utter nonsense and defies all possible logic: we all live in the same world, all live and breathe the same air. We all live our lives to the best of our abilities and survive in what is in fact a hallucinogenic labyrinth and we keep on moving back and forth endlessly. We get out of breath, we get into trouble, and we become the ultimate enemy, the germ, the microbe entering inside anyone's body.

The enemy gets inside us anyway, no matter what. We don't need to be out of breath but when we are at our lowest point, we are more vulnerable. The viruses will turn anyone into someone we wish we would have never become: the beggar: the filth, the weak, the rat or the mouse crawling around on the ground.

The journey may feel like a skein of thread in a tangle but it's not unfathomable and certainly not impossible to navigate throughout; it just needs some getting used to it and years of practice.

I got caught in a circle of hell and became a virus entering someone's body. I became a rat and lived into the far end of the gutter. I've lived with my fellow rats and mice in the streets of London. Wherever I went, I left some marks in order to later in time draw a map, a map of the universe. This is how I escape the world, in between dimensions:

The **Negative dimension** is a three-dimensional space: a geometric setting in which three values: parameters are required to determine the position of an element (i.e., point). This is the informal meaning of the term dimension. The world consists of two dimensions: The Positive and the Negative. The Negative dimension is like an unprocessed side of what used to be a photographic picture.

The Positive dimension is the world in full colour where we are supposed to live. In reality we're not. We live in the Negative. We never die there.

Thousands of years of living creatures are all living in the Negative dimension. It's never ending whereas in the Positive dimension, we only have one life.

My first encounter with G, Gordon Griffith as he told me

he was called on that fated 14 September 2007, when I was living at the Deauville Hotel, 103 E 29th St, New York, NY 10016, United States off Park Avenue, inside a very classy room, large ceiling with just the space for a double bed, a large sink, a large square mirror above the sink and space for toiletries. The shower is on the same floor, one needs to share the bathroom. There was a very large window, the size of the room with a view over the street and the opposite building, from the 4th floor. There was a TV but I have never been very keen on it, so I gave it a miss.

Every day I used to stroll around Park Avenue from one opposite end to the other, from Union square to the MetLife Building, a skyscraper at Park Avenue and 45th Street, north of Grand Central Terminal, in Midtown Manhattan. I have been to New York before, as a kid but it was in 1982, at Saint Marks Place, Avenue D in East Village at the height of the New Wave scene. Life was perhaps equally desperate but full of hope and extremely vibrant.

This time around, trends and fashion have all but died off and I ended up on Park Avenue, completely oblivious of what went on, between the offices of Madoff and Whole Foods, 4 Union Square E, New York, NY 10003, United States and Brian Epstein, The Credit Suisse building on a street off Park Avenue, 11 Madison Avenue, New York, NY 10010, infamous for the biggest amount of money laundering New York had to offer. I have never been out in the evening. I just stayed at the hotel which had a very engaging lobby with armchairs and sofa, a room with a piano where I had plenty of time to practice and compose new music and a computer room where I would pick up my emails every day.

The main lift was very much stuck in the 1920s, just like the rest of the building and needed a lift man or a lift woman to operate the wheel.

Every day, I ate and bought my food from the extremely expensive and pretentious Whole Foods store on Union Square and I spent most afternoons reading books in my bed, generally bought from Barnes and Noble at 33 E 17th St, New York, NY 10003, United States. The piano practice was reserved for the mornings.

This is with all this backdrop that I first met with G, sitting on the pavements, like the depraved, destitute and shivering hobo that he was then under the pouring rain. The coincidences of life are a very mysterious science.

I do not recall having met G before, just on that fateful day and that precise moment in time. There he was, a broken man of 16 or 18 years old or even 20, very hard to tell from his face but certainly in an appalling state, he could barely afford a smile with his crooked teeth, lost at least 3 at first glance, wearing an old coat and a blanket over his shoulders.

I hate it when I see people living like that; it gets me really angry and I feel the urge to step in.

I suspect that it must be subconscious for fear of ending up in the streets like them.

I told him that he cannot stay here otherwise he would be sick and worse. He agreed but stated that he has nowhere else to go.

I then told him that he must come with me and he did so promptly. We stopped at Whole Foods
4 Union Square E, New York, NY 10003, for a bite to eat. He sat in the ugly decorated dining area, not fussing about what I would bring him but nevertheless, he requested a hot chocolate.

I failed to ask if he ate meat or not, I suspected that he did - I do not- so I bought some chicken and veg.

He ate everything at the speed of light but took some time to savour his hot chocolate.

He noticed my plate of vegetables. He asked: "Where's the meat?" and I replied that "I do not eat any, or even fish".

He then stared at me for a few seconds then I broke the attack by glancing the best smile I could generate to him and he then broke his attack with the best smile he could offer, albeit broken.

"I couldn't live without meat. I prefer my meat raw". This comment was uncalled for and made me hesitate, whilst he started to tell me about his story, to invite him to my hotel.

I then explained to him a few facts of life and a few rules about staying in the hotel, just in case he would start thrashing the hotel. Mind you and unlike what it has been said, the Sex Pistols only stayed a short while at the Chelsea hotel but they stayed the longest at the Deauville hotel and even then, they smashed the hotel. Just for the record, it's Sid Vicious and his girlfriend Nancy who lived at the Chelsea hotel and died there.

I told him that I would bring him some new clothes in the morning.

I felt this urge to ascertain the situation. We must have spent an hour at Whole Foods, time for him to visit the restroom and me to fetch him another hot chocolate whilst he was otherwise engaged.

It was nearly 10 pm, closing time and we were both exhausted. I asked him if he could walk 15 minutes and he said that he could, so we both trotted along to the Deauville hotel. Once we arrived, we stealthily scuttled up the stairs to the fourth floor fearing that his scruffy state might deny him entry and I then asked him to sit on a chair in the corridor whilst I organised him a room.

I managed to explain to the duty receptionist that a friend will come later and I needed to book him a room. I got the key and this time used the lift, the duty receptionist became the liftman and we both arrived on the 4th floor. Thankfully he departed straight away and has not seen my new found friend.

In the morning, G slept until midday so I had plenty of time to buy him some clothes and bring him back some lunch.

As the days went by, I organised a dentist for him from the homeless list that I picked up from a local church but still needed to pay about $400 for 3 teeth. Good teeth (good smile) and good elocution is paramount for anyone trying to return to the land of the living. One needs to be looked at, then be able to interact. No one would look at a defined ugly face.

We talked, every day and every day until he regained more strength and felt more assertive. It went on for two weeks. He told me about his life, his upbringing and the reason why he was forced to run away to New York.

As his life story so far unfolded, I got more and more fascinated until after the second week when he really became more assertive, arrogant and cocksure about himself and also asked to eat some raw meat, red meat as that.

I agreed and bought him some. From then on, and every day until the last week, a series of gruesome stories will emerge. Stories that will churn anyone's stomach but didn't reach me in that sense. I remain unfazed and detached from it all.

I have always possessed this uncanny capacity to transport myself in another dimension in the face of adversity and impossible situations. Daydreaming, one might say. Whilst being able to smile or nod my head, I can vanish somewhere else and blank anything. However, anything else is still recorded in my brain and resurfaces later. In impossible situations, my subconscious acted for me to avoid being embarrassed or panicked. It would have been catastrophic if G lost my confidence and empathy.

I have been left, bewildered, stranded and empty-handed but having had this ability to freeze in time (and not showing it). This saved me from worse and death.

At the end of the second week, G collapsed on the pavements, screaming in deep agony. His pain was excruciating. I think it was a tumour deeply rooted, although I have never been able to ascertain this with the doctors. He died 48 hours later at the hospital.

I have never been able to say goodbye and never seen him again, not even his dead body. I have asked the doctors and nurses at the hospital if I could organise a funeral but I have been told that the "authorities" will deal with it.

Somehow, I did not feel the urge to complain or challenge this decision and left, being in a hallucinating state, even more bewildered and dumbfounded than I have been during our daily sessions. Who is G -Gordon Griffin-? Is he really called Gordon Griffin? Was his entire life story so far, the product of some fertile imagination?

What I have witnessed was his insatiable appetite for raw meat and in his general manners, a certain sadism has clearly emerged.

He was born in a suburb of Ann Arbor, a city in Michigan, his parents never lived together but he lived with his father. He believed he had four brothers, as far as he could remember but they got separated when he was 2 and they

have been sent to a foster home. His mom was sent to a
"loony bin". He had trouble at school as he couldn't
understand anything and the teachers couldn't be
bothered. They were 30, on average in the classroom. "Too
crowded" and "too noisy" to learn anything. His father
took him to a Baptist church every Sunday. He lived in a
two-bedroom apartment on the outskirts of –and if the
coincidences of life aren't so weird- in a suburb of Ann
Arbor, a city in Michigan. Just like Roosevelt. The
apartment had a tiny kitchen and very old as that, a tiny
bathroom with a bath and everything was filthy since no
one cleaned anything.

His father was very strict. He was in bed by 7 pm and
must be up at 6 am every day until he decided to run away
from his home. If he was late for school or displeased his
father, he was forced over his bed, backwards, his trousers
and underwear down and brutally thrashed with his
father's belt or a whip and they had many whips in the
house; the kind used for horses. He can't recall a day
without being thrashed. I told him that it was impossible
to endure such a treatment every day.

Why didn't he mention it to his teachers, his priest or his
doctor? His father knew them all well. It was a small town,
so it would have been worse. He got thrashed many times
by his main teacher just for being in the classroom but the
teacher would thrash anyone. The priest thrashed him too
because his father told him that he needed to be
disciplined.

G told me that: "My father would often make me stand
underneath a cold shower for a few minutes before

thrashing so that the blows will hurt more but it will leave less marks on my bare buttocks. Sometimes he fell into a state of anger and he would not stop and the more I pleaded with him and the more he thrashed my ass. It felt like it lasted at least half an hour. I then was allowed to lie down on my stomach to heal the wounds until I fell asleep. I often touched my buttocks and the blood was all over my hands. This only happened when I felt like it lasted for 30 minutes."

The more a person will endure the pain and the more the person would either want more pain or would become more insensitive towards any suffering. It becomes a routine and the mind's belief is that it is a necessary routine. G remembered that he was still in his nappies and his father would remove them and spank his buttocks then leaving him alone in the locked bathroom to cry. Becoming an adult, the victim would want either someone else to suffer or find someone to continue this routine and feel the pain on a daily basis and it is no longer an ordeal but a necessity craving to find or create.

The reason I've only approached two men rather than young girls or women in the streets, it's just that it is just impossible. For a woman to end up in the streets is somehow an even more catastrophic situation and they never last long. They are either rescued by specialised agencies or rescued by pimps and other gangsters.

I have never attempted to help or even talked to a girl on the streets and I have rarely ever seen any. She might accept an invitation then panic then, it's like if I was "picking up" a girl from the streets. Grooming is the word.

Men are different and I've rarely done it as I normally just slip them some money and I do not believe they would make bad use of it like all the homeless agencies are saying. Even if they buy drugs, at least that would keep them happy for a short moment in time. In the case of G and Roosevelt, I got literally attracted by their appalling state. Not in a sexual way, far from it but there was a mystery that attracted me to them.

There was something I needed to know and I had to find out.

My mom was raped and this was my conception and I do not regard rape very lightly. I researched it and G was perhaps the extension to my research.

In my film Speed of Light, there is a character called G1. I never actually realised why I called Gordon G again, perhaps simply because the first letter of his name was G. In Speed of Light, my character was a down and out that has spent some time in an abandoned warehouse and he dreams about meeting his imaginary girlfriend and then forces himself on him. We spent months before the filming trying to work out the scene and I had opted out for them to narrate the scene separately over the footage of the house. They didn't like the idea and the producers refused.

They physically had sex using some of the text I gave them. I didn't find this good or gruesome, just stupid.

The scene has been uploaded by the assistant director on several websites and I found it revolting. The film couldn't get a lower rating than 18 in the UK or R in America, the

DVD with subtitles in 6 languages in 4 formats sold exceedingly well and the album soundtrack went gold. I have never had such success since the eighties. To crown the whole thing, I divided a sound catalogue with 300 ringtones, car alarms and door bells using images of Speed of Light and other films as a backdrop that went everywhere in the world and sold many millions and in those days, the days being 2008 and directly with phone companies as opposed to the main monopoly of a few Silicon companies' websites that we have today that constantly fiddle the figures so they don't have to pay much to anyone.

I didn't feel so well that the film went well. The film actually didn't work, people bought it because of that "infamous" scene". It was revolting. When the film was then split up in scenes and uploaded on YouTube, I tried very hard to explain the scene so that people could understand and set off some limits and alarms. The chances for this to be seen are nil since on YouTube view counts start on an editorial process and it needs to be "funny" and "idiotic" or a song launched by a young mainstream artist. Anything else will mean that the clip will be marked as near X and the user will need to login reducing the chances to be seen, just like the rest of the film. On the back of this I moved to New York and my way not to stay too idle was to bump into G and Roosevelt. The coincidences of life where we have been drawn together from very different horizons in the streets of New York are indeed a very mysterious science.

When drug addicts are sent into recovery, they are all assembled together and they kick off the addiction together. I suppose all people who have been abused end up meeting someone else that has been abused. I'm not sure if it is a subconscious therapy since many abused ends up abusing as a result -and I'm not defending this- it is bewildering to be drawn to such people.

Most serial killers and monsters are men but there were a few women like Myra Stewart in the sixties in England, who committed unmentionable acts against children and always refused to say where the bodies were.

I think with most women who are violent, there is a mother instinct that at some point kicks in and slows them down. There is no such thing in men. I know it is clichéd that in the film Monster, Charlize Theron portrays a monster and she was a lesbian, type casting lesbians from being all violent and brutal, as opposed to the weak and obedient woman, servile to her husband.

In my film The Y2K File, someone, whilst searching the web, discovered the story of an ogre who kidnapped a woman and had many children and ate them all -we are venturing to the extreme here-. Such a story existed, as I found it on the web in 1999 and in 2008 there was a similar story about an ogre -a man- in Austria who did the same thing. I do not believe that these are isolated incidents and it's more urgent than ever to have proper functioning agencies and government agencies that acts promptly when someone goes missing, when a child is beaten up at home, when a child has bruises in any parts of his body or when someone has been raped.

These things should never happen but they do because of

the failure to report, too scared that our lives will be messed up as a result or simply for fear of being questioned by the authorities and very often to be brushed off by the police. Most women never report a rape for fear of re-living it all by violent questions from the police and the authorities. That in the 21st century our authorities have not established ways to welcome the victims of such a crime in a way that will not make them the one who caused this, is beyond comprehension.

There is currently no real protection for children or women anywhere in the world and certainly no pre-emptive ways to educate. We are slowly normalising rape and violence against children and women.

Following my mother's rape by two men, one being her own father, my grandfather -so I have officially two biological fathers and the process to find all this out has taken officially 30 years-, she was never been the same again, her life has been completely broken and was unable to look after me and I have instead been fostered by her sister, my aunt and her husband who became a severe and brutal alcoholic.

My aunt's husband once followed me with a sharp cooking knife around our apartment whilst he was possessed with his usual rage whilst without any alcohol and compensating for it by committing violent acts. As I was rushing through the front door, the owner of the apartment building above stood on the doorstep, panicked by all the screaming and all the noises. Seeing my aunt's husband with a knife in his hand and me bleeding profusely with my nose in pieces, he ordered the monster to stop and grabbed me and drove me to the nearest hospital. Even if the staff took care of me, it never removed the physical and mental pain and the pain of having to be interrogated by social services.

At least I wasn't alone. There were times when I had found refuge inside the bathroom but he would kick the door like a maniac without tiring and it must have gone on for an hour. Only when I felt he might have collapsed and finally exhausted, I would nervously open the door and run to my bedroom nearby and run away through the window. At least we were on the ground floor, otherwise I would have been killed jumping out of the window and in those days, I thought about killing myself many times and indeed I did try.

On that day when I ran away and when I stopped in a park, I cried for hours on end asking myself why this was happening, why was I here and why did I deserve this? I was alone there. If in Tibetan philosophy they say that we are born alone and die alone, I really believe that we also grow up and live alone.

No children deserve to be kicked, smashed and brutalised in this way. In fact, no human being or other members of the animal kingdom must be subjected to such a horror.

I often think and actually believe that everyone is to blame. Everyone is to blame. Everyone covers for everyone's crimes. Everyone is scared to say anything, by fear of the implications, fear to attract problems, so we cover. We are scared but we are all responsible.

Everyone wants to live a peaceful and prosperous life, so best not get involved. One is born to be abused and one is a born abuser; except that the role often changes and the abused may turn up to be an abuser in order to seek revenge.

I do call the abusers monsters or beasts but I also sympathised with them. Killing these people won't serve any purpose, the damage has been done. We can only try to remove further damage and if re-education is futile, we could consider surgery. Psychosurgery (in the brain) has never worked so far and too often abused and used to silence someone politically, so it needs to be regulated. For serial rapists, there is only chemical castration, if other treatments fail.

My aunt's husband was a severe alcoholic, so why is alcohol still on sale? I never liked it and there could be a connection but I'm very against this. Who has allowed all the drugs in the county? Why do we allow people to become addicts? Why do people feel the need to be addicted to cope in this life that we live?

Even without rape, the conception is a violent act. Sex is violent and the birth even more so for the mother.

My mother tried to hide her baby -that was me- even as she got bigger, pretending that she put on weight. She gave birth on her own and I would hate to imagine how catastrophic it must have been. I often wondered about how it happened. Who cut the umbilical cord? I hope there wasn't any blood. The neighbour got curious when she

heard a baby crying and came in and eventually my
mother was driven to hospital.

My granddad knew all about the conception since he was
present. He tried to get rid of the baby but failed. Abortion
wasn't a solution. My grandfather even organised a trip to
the mountain and forced her to ski and couldn't ski and
even if she stated that she wasn't feeling well -two weeks
before I was due- she went along. My uncle remembered
as I asked him if she fell and replied so casually that yes,
she did a few times, she couldn't ski. She drunk a lot,
mainly in the evening during her pregnancy and drunk
loads of coffee each day with at least 2 packets of cigarettes
to get through the trauma of having been raped. I'm
amazed that I didn't turn up to be a heroin addict, an
alcoholic or even a heavy smoker.

As far as my aunt's husband, as I have mentioned before. I
just blank the whole episode. I remembered what
happened but it's just that since everyone went on with
their own life as normal, I must have subconsciously
assumed that it was normal. Only 20 years later when I
first mentioned what happened to some friends what
happened that they were horrified and this transposition
made me remember about the pain and how I used to run
away and cry for hours or the episode when he couldn't
stop punching me and my I thought my heart stopped
beating or beating too fast in a similar way that I have felt
when I contracted tinnitus. It feels like you were hearing
noises inside your head when in fact the noises are coming
through the ears and when the punching stopped, I could
hear the heart beating so fast that it reverberated all
through the night.

What saved me is that somehow, I felt this urge at some
point to fight back and even retaliated and when he chased
me around the apartment, threw some chairs over his face.
The only way to fight back and I used to scream extremely
loudly and this attracted the neighbour. As a result, I
develop an angry itch when I feel threatened and can
become extremely angry. I never let this anger turn into
violence but anger triggers violence. The whole
mechanism is absolutely scary.

Both G and Roosevelt, the two characters in my story, have
both been plagued by tinnitus. I diagnosed it with G and
Roosevelt told me. It is rather obvious that they have both
contracted tinnitus because of the violence. For me, it may
have been there but it didn't manifest itself until it got
triggered when it actually started when I called my bank
back in 2014, a bank that was using overseas call centres in
ISIS occupied Syria and a bomb detonated during our
conversation to my left ear. The sound should have been
muffled through the phone line but it could have been the
reverberation. The end result was that as soon as I replaced
the handset. I heard violent noises inside my head and I
soon realised that for at least a week I became completely
deaf. The sheer coincidences of life were to be forced to
endure a forced conversation at the mercy of an ISIS
member. ISIS is known for its extreme violence and that is
another story.

I wonder if in life we are drawn to violence or being
confronted to violence.

Unlike many children who have been abused and sexually

abused, I have never felt the urge to seek revenge. It's not actually certain that all victims seek revenge but by having an outcome, a court case, a trial and a verdict, it seems that the pain may finally rest. Otherwise, the pain and trauma remain here until the day you die.

I have always felt revulsion towards psychologists and psychiatrists. I really believe that they are dangerous individuals. They either chose this profession in the vain hope to solve their own problems or are abusers themselves in disguise. It is not regulated. A verdict by a psychiatrist, as badly conceived as possible, can destroy someone's life. My aunt had a degree in psychology, she was bi polar and had many other health problems. She has been abused by her father as a child and he was also extremely violent. She told me that she preferred when her mom (second wife) "whipped them as it was less brutal". When I heard such a thing, it really enraged me.

When questioned by the psy(s), I really felt that I was going to be punished for daring to expose this violent situation. They never helped anyway, so what was the point?

The reason social services failed to remove me from the abusive relationship is exactly what G said when I asked him why the teacher, priest etc. failed to act or even if they pretended to be acting, they would soon shut down the process: "They all know each other".

There is a survival instinct with any abuse and it's to keep it secret -at least for as long as possible- for fear that it could become worse.

At least the abuse, kept secret, can always be construed - for anyone concerned and including the abused- as normal and blank it and ignore it and it then becomes a necessary process of growing up.

I really need to state that I firmly believe that we need to define each protagonist for what they are: the abuser and the abused and not the "victim" as everyone can claim to be a victim and it has lost its meaning.

On the second week of our daily interviews with G, it became pure torture. Listening to every detail from G, from his fondness of raw meat and how he started to eat human flesh was taking its toll. I survived this ordeal by my power of escapism that I have often used as a child. I learnt to remain stoic and unfazed with this ability to daydream during a conversation or impossible situation and be transported somewhere else, in a different dimension as far away as possible.

It somehow saved me and saved me as I couldn't panic and needed to keep a brave face and keep on smiling when I needed to smile as I didn't want to end up eaten alive.

I may have been "away" when he confided in me what happened to him and what this led to. but my memory was there and came back when I needed to access it and for this process to work, I best need to be on my own. I re-used the six "murders" G committed in T.

I became convinced that he really did commit the murders. I have also been convinced that murders and cannibalism

are more frequent than is commonly acknowledged and it
may be rampant. After all, thousands or hundreds of
thousands of people go missing around the world and
never reappear.

I wrote and directed the opera, murder, mystery and
thriller The Y2K file, largely based on the story of Myra
Hindley and her partner in the sixties in England when
they kidnapped, tortured and sexually assaulted children
to death. All this convinced me to work on this and her
unmentionable cruelty against children and beyond
cruelty because even in jail she has always refused to say
when some of the children have been buried.

It was also based on the news back in 2007 in Austria
about an ogre who kidnapped a woman for many years,
fathered her many children and then ate some of the
children.

It has been seen through the eyes of an 18 years' old man
who lost his family in a fire that devastated the family
home and tried to make sense of it all, alone in an
abandoned house haunted by an ogre who once lived in
the house and left deep down in the basement, a bunker,
the mutilated children.

When the film was completed, it couldn't go through the
censors in England and could only be seen for the over 18.

I have asked 22 friends, acquaintances and the actors in the
film and their friends to view the film. Even though they
found the film and story well-made and original, only a
few could find the film agonising as much as I did. I

waited 10 years before releasing the film and even then, I did it very slowly, by releasing it as an audio soundtrack album and also released 13 singles with an image of each chapter as a cover.

It's crucial that horror and cruelty be told for others to retell the story and know.

Much more must be done. It's not to glamorising it; it's for everyone to know the signs and to know how to react and how to prevent it. It does seem too incredible that it can take years before anyone; an ogre, serial killer or beast be caught and that anyone could possibly act like this with impunity and that no one can stop it even caught in a vicious circle of covering it, ignoring it for fear of being involved, for fear that others may wrongly label the person who tries to prevent or report such crimes.

In Burning from the Inside, I have been given the opportunity between 1997 and 2003 to interview over 101 members of a Nigerian tribe in an extremely volatile region where oil is being extracted causing untold environmental damage, where the Nigerian army routinely burn down the houses from the people who disagree, where women are routinely raped by soldiers and gangsters and where gay men or lesbians can be burnt alive if caught. Again, such horrendous horrors exist but no one wants to see it.

The presentation may have been hampered by me, as I have been accused by many to sabotage its final presentation, but wanted the film to be in black and white. For me, the only white person amongst a sea of black

Africans, it was a necessity. I have found their outstanding faces and courage transpiring more deeply in black and white. One person that I have interviewed had half of his face slit and the day before, along with some local militia, kidnapped over 30 Nigerians on an oil rig, off the coast of Nigeria and nearly all of the hostages have been killed. I have just been told a few seconds before he has come to me for the interview.

Documentary filmmaking is like movie making, to make it work, one needs to create scenes or situations that are not real, there needs to be some fiction to be believed as non-fiction. When in the case of Burning from the Inside or The Y2K File, it becomes too real and far too horrendous for the brain to control, let alone digest and the audience will not cope and run away. There is a reality that is far too frightening to handle.

During that time in 2000, I had this idea of locking 12 contestants for a pilot reality show in the dark, with cameras everywhere but the night vision cameras needed to be black out of white and this again was a turn off for the producers. Green night vision could have been ok but not black out of white of black and white night cams, a no-go area. The content also became too much to handle as we filmed them sleeping, having a shower or eating the meal that we provided to them. The rules were that they needed to stay in the dark for a month in order to win. However, this ordeal turned out to be short lived and no one made it for more than a week, over 400 hours of footage has been archived.

Each day there would be sessions where they would be

interviewed and audited with a K thermometer, a Kelvin measurement to assess the high frequency of the brain (and the mind).

Humans are far too afraid of the dark. Some believe that forcing someone in the dark can cure any ailments, addictions, mass murderers and rapists.

I called it the "Est" (For electric shock treatment) experiment.

Since the experience has been short lived, we will never know if it really works.

In 2023, we restored 2 hours' worth of footage, divided the piece in small chapters and made it available online under the title of "Between Time and Space".

Why one gets attracted to interview people and listen to what they have to say is a mystery. Perhaps it is in order to know oneself better, to crave the opportunity to know from others how to behave or not to behave.

It seems that it became a lifelong job or antidote. When I have embarked on over 300 interviews with my producer James Hogan, a top 10 City advisor With Brunswick, the consultancy firm, and also advised 3 Prime Ministers and members of the Royal family, there seems to be no end on who we could interview.

Sometimes on audio and some on video. We worked with the Edinburgh Business School and interviewed CEOs of British businesses. We interviewed top government advisors and one of the key people accused of causing the 2008 financial crisis. The hour-long interview revolved around mental health as he was now championing this, in his forced retirement.

Anyone causing disasters, serial murderers, serial rapists and monsters all hide themselves when caught into the mirage of mental health. **Get on with it!** Everyone may be a victim and a sufferer but, in that case, no one can help since everyone is suffering and needs treatment and the world is set to collapse because people will often abuse each other and kill one another.

We can seek help but the help on offer turns things for the worse. In the absence of real and functioning therapy, we can only get on with it and no one can help better than oneself; we are all alone in this world especially when the unspeakable and unmentionable has been committed.

One must get on with it! Except that I struggle with this and I still want to change the world. We need to have alarm bells, non-judgmental and unbiased help. Be able to confess, to be stopped or be guided. By doing this we would be pre-emptive and avoid the worst. Somehow, we got so beyond this, the human race seems to even rejoice in all. We don't prosecute anymore, prisons are overcrowded, extreme violence is omnipresent in the streets and we have even managed to normalise and even legalised rape.

In France, in the news, there was a guy arrested for being a "mule" -someone who carried cocaine for a dealer. When he was arrested and in court -before being jailed- in his defence, he said that he couldn't feed his family or get help

-which is true since it has been verified-.

People die on drugs. Why do we allow a situation like this to occur? There are no alarm bells, no one to cry for help. So, everyone does what one has to do, no matter the consequences, no matter if people die.

What is beyond surprising is that we even jail the killer in the first place. Of course, there is a huge cost to it -never mind about the loss of life, it has been done- the huge cost to the taxpayer not to mention the families of all victims.

There is a dark logic in all this that is astounding!
I rest my case.

Chapter Two: Roosevelt and Me.

Franklin Roosevelt was born in Little Rock, Arkansas. Absent father, he ended up in the care of his mother who hated him. His mother was a heavy smoker, drank coffee all day but didn't drink.

Roosevelt believed that his birth was the result of an accident or a rape since her mother hated men: she always screamed at him, telling him that all men are the lowest of the low. He never knew if his mother loved women since she behaved extremely violently with them. Once there was a cousin of hers at the house and she punched her and she fell over the floor. She brutalised her youngest sister as well but even though they always came back to the tiny apartment they were living in.

Roosevelt told me that: "He had 3 rooms and at first, I slept inside my mother's room and it's when as a baby, I used to spank him for crying or for no apparent reasons. When I was two, she dragged me over the floor and punched me in the stomach. Her sister was there and although my mom's sister would have helped me and checked if I was alright, she instead had to deal with my mother and had a violent argument. "

From then on Roosevelt was placed in the third room, a tiny cupboard, the second room was the living room. Then the punishments never stopped and when he was ill or crying, he was horse whipped with a leather belt Age, age 5 and his mother came in one afternoon with a wooden stick and ordered me to lie down over his bed without any clothes on and she walloped his backside so violently that he bled and bled profusely. It seemed to him that it went on for an hour, excruciating pain always felt like it but it only stopped when the neighbours alerted by his screams barged inside the apartment and inside the room and were confronted with the mother in full action. When the neighbour tried to stop her, she whipped them but one neighbour managed to call the police, but by the time she arrived, some of the neighbours and Roosevelt himself were in such a state that they all had to be rushed to hospital. Roosevelt stayed in hospital for a month, the mother was rightfully jailed and it was the last he had heard of her.

Roosevelt was then sent to an orphanage, all the way to Ann Harbor, Michigan, for two years, a very uneventful time where he did not make any friends or exchange with anyone but where at least, he was given the peace and the time to heal. learn to write and by 7 he has been sent to another orphanage then to a foster dad. The absence of a wife or female is unusual for foster parents but the man was an ex-military officer and a nurse.

Although not often there, the foster carer was kind and helpful and encouraged him with his schooling and even achieved good grades in High school.

There was no love as in a loving home but a peaceful home. Roosevelt never forged any friendship in school, has been well brought up, strict but not too militarized and certainly no violence.

When he was 18, his foster carer died suddenly and distant cousins came in, emptied the house, and emptied Roosevelt himself. He was forced to leave, his small bag with him containing some clothes and a few books. He barely had any money, just some pocket money. One bright morning of spring, he spent half a day wandering in the streets, pondering where he should go. He stopped at a Greyhound coach station.

He browsed all the journeys advertised on a board and saw New York. New York sounded big and promising and had just enough for the fare. He spent a few days travelling, sleeping, reading and dreaming of a future life in New York.

On arrival, full of hope, without any money and no map, he
travelled along the streets of Manhattan. He ended up on Union
Square, he saw it mentioned somewhere in the past
and there he was. The food market was all there and thriving, he
was hungry and could barely afford a sandwich.

Some say that there are no coincidences in life and it all happens
for a reason. He gave up eating meat when he was 10. He never
liked meat. His foster carer never minded and that's how he
brought himself up. On that day, precisely at noon, I heard him
asking the vendor if he had no meat in his sandwich and the
vendor confirmed it. I overheard this and glanced around and
smiled at Roosevelt and he smiled back at me. I then moved
further down and sat over a bench to tidy up some papers and
there he was sitting next to me.

We couldn't avoid looking at each other and he then said that
New York is such a big city.

I never liked asking where people come from or if people asked
me but I felt this urge to ask him, there was something incredible
about him, I felt compelled to ask where he came from.

He did tell me and I then asked what he was doing in New York.
He then started crying, howling and he was uncontrollable. He
must have cried for an hour. I then went to him, hugged him and
he was deeply shocked and told me that no one has ever hugged
him before. I can't recall ever having been hugged by my aunt or
her husband when I was living with them so in that sense, I
wasn't surprised. I took him to Whole Foods and we had tea and
biscuits.

It was the first of 32 days of continuous friendship. He would tell
me about himself and his upbringing and I would tell him about
myself.

I booked him to my hotel and fed him, paid for him. Roosevelt

had a dream to start university, learn social science and become
a politician. His own way of trying to change the world. He also
dreamed of finding a wife and having children, creating a family
that he never had and being a loving father to his children and
loving husband.

As the days unfolded, I also had so much paperwork to sort out,
he became a real asset and my assistant.

We tried to work out ways for him to start a university course
and the funding. He never had to fill in a form before and I did,
and became specialised at it. Applying for lottery funding or tax
credits in England, and doing so for two decades, the only way
to succeed, one becomes a master in the art of filling a form.

Unbeknownst to him, I wrote part of his story in, not the
gruesome and revolting part but essentially being a near orphan.

Roosevelt got offered a place at a NY university and funding for
the course, he told me it was the happiest day of his life. He
cried and cried the whole Niagara Falls, just like the day I met
him, only this time I hope that they were tears of happiness. and
this time he hugged me and hugged me so much that I fell over
the floor but it was a very happy fall.

I never saw Roosevelt again but we exchanged emails and he is
married with two children, a boy and a girl and apparently, he
named the boy Nick after me, sent me some pictures and has
entered politics.

I really would like to believe that he will be the best politician
that has ever existed in America and the best father that has ever
lived on planet Earth.

As always, I do not tend to get attached with anyone. I travel
and move from places to places and try to create a living with
my art and each time, it is a new adventure each time as painful

as the previous one, as life needs to be exposed and publicised so that someone, somewhere will know and it may help someone to survive in the most brutal, egotistic and cruel world the universe has possibly created.

Dr Joseph writes in his enthralling book The Right Brain and the Unconscious that a child is always a child and even if a teen or adult, the child part of human development will always be there. He compared the child in humans to the trees when they grow: "The young tree that once was, never disappears. The central core -the child- will always be there". If we were to root out this core -referring to the tree- the tree will die".

If the central core is weak and diseased, then no matter how expert the core, the adult tree will be as feeble as its foundation. Just as the living tree retains its early core, within the core of each of us is the child that we once were. This child constitutes the foundation of what we have become, who we are, and what we will be".

Although millions of people suffer from gruesome abuses - myself included- not everyone ends up becoming a mass murderer or a monster and I believe that I have not become one and far from it.

Food and malnutrition also come into the development of a child and will later impair judgment and cognitive performance and it's extremely hard and almost impossible to reverse the process.

I may not be the brightest of all people but I have an extremely strong sense of taste and smell and I can smell my fruits and vegetables and define them by my taste if it is deemed edible. The same process goes with the touch and I will also run a mile if I see an "inflated veg" (high in pesticides) and this will without a shadow of a doubt create a major chemical imbalance in the body and ultimately damage the brain.

The old adage is beyond true: "we are what we eat". My foster parents knew how to eat well and I never suffered from deficiencies on that score. Sadly, it is hardly the case for millions, even billions of humans on planet Earth.

My way of running away was to use my extremely fertile imagination and my readings. One of my favourite subjects is dark matter. My dark matter may be a form of escapism but it's real and lawyers and dimensions of horrors and cruelty from different times live side by side. I wouldn't want to be a time traveller, star trekking through dimensions and living one nightmare to the next.

Dark matter is a form of matter accounting for about 85% of the universe and about a quarter of its total energy density. It was first acknowledged throughout astrophysical observations, including gravitational effects that cannot be explained. It has been called "dark" as it cannot be detected by standard astrological tools. It is thought to be referred to as the "negative dimension" as opposed to the "positive dimension" that we all live in and therefore must contain a form of life that defies gravity. It has been assumed since the dawn of mankind that the "mind" and "spirit" travels there as soon as the body becomes mortal, fuelling the possibility that a completely different universe exists within completely undefinable parameters.

The perception of reality has different views: we either see nothing, so it is completely black or completely white. Then we try to furnish this empty space and add memories and figments of our imagination. It becomes colourful as this universe so created has layers and layers of landscapes intertwined with all the sounds our mind recorded during our lifetime so far juxtaposed in the background shaping into one giant noise. This noise is omnipresent: it helps us to remain sane and together with the layers of landscape, they build a world and a story so we won't be afraid of emptiness

The Positive and Negative dimensions fuelled by many lawyers in between. The Negative dimension is a three-dimensional space: a geometric setting in which three values: parameters are required to determine the position of an element (i.e., point). This is the informal meaning of the term dimension. The world consists of two dimensions: The Positive and the Negative. The Negative dimension is like an unprocessed side of what used to be a photographic picture. The Positive is the world in full colour where we are supposed to live. In reality we're not. We live in the Negative. We never die there. Thousands of years of living creatures are all living in the Negative dimension. It's never ending whereas in the Positive dimension, we only have one life.

I have spent all my life researching dark matter -dimensions: first, second and third all living side by side; centuries of atrocities.

In terms of atrocities, one cannot ignore genocides and the Holocaust. War is different as somehow, I'm of the belief that there are other ways to resolve problems but wars are a huge business.

I can't stand adults engaging in violence but as long as it is consenting S&M, so even if wars revolt me, I only put a stand if there are children involved.

I have two great uncles who died in the Holocaust. It is still unreal that so many people ignore
the facts of it:

As I was browsing and searching for the Holocaust, I came across JewishGen.org. The main introduction goes:

"At JewishGen, we look at the past, and try to reclaim the memory of what was. But by itself, memories are not enough. We can't live in the past, and we can't reclaim it. But we can allow the memories of the past to shape us, to shape our sense of identity, and to shape what we will be transmitting to future generations."

I would say that the past is never dead and always returns when we're least expecting it. A Holocaust scholar, Yehuda Bower, suggested three more commandments to the original ten of Moses's: "Thou shalt not be a perpetrator or victim and thou shalt never ever be a bystander".

The real story of wars is also the years and decades that follow, all the days the wounded and bereaved survivors have to struggle through only to bequeath the anguish to other generations. I'm not sure if I agree with this. The past is the present and the future combined. It is the present tense.

Chapter Three: Violence in the language.

In 2019, I came across three "children" of about 10-14 of age and I walked slowly behind them and listened to every word. They were discussing what someone and it can't possibly be them but referring to what some adults, I hope, had done to a gay man and a woman. In terms of film making, I always try to depict the contemporary and it is highly primordial to do so, just like in Godard's films. Nothing to do with being vulgar but a film is there to either entertain or to inform. A film is a witness of events that occurred, has yet to come and must never be and films can warn about reality.

I remembered word for word the incredible sordid dialogue and was somehow more frightened by the brutal evolution of the language rather than its content. The content became more real when we used that scene for the Prologue and the Epilogue to a film that has been banned.

The way we rendered it was very simple; we asked one actor, James Waterhouse, to tell the whole screenplay to someone. As the rehearsal unfolded onto the final take, let's just say that the actor was brilliant in his rendition. The trouble is, I thought it was beyond anything imaginable. James orated the dialogue in one go with brilliant eloquence and speed. Ten members of my team and friends viewed this, some nearly laughed or smirked in front of the aberration of this rendition. It was absurd, it is absurd but real!

The producers and the Ladies in the film, Janet and Jane were adamant that we had to keep it as it is, Janet being very feminist

thought that we could go ahead and it will have a major impact
in the positive direction. When I submitted the screenplay to the
British Film Institute as we needed to in order to receive some
funding, the Head of the certification, Anna Mansi went berserk.
She asked us to warn her in advance before submitting such a
screenplay. We did and it was marked in red "Warning". It
triggered a deplorable war of words between her, Janet and
myself that should have never happened but did and caused us
to lose the funding on this film but also on any other films.

The situation in Britain is catastrophic and now the children in
schools are doing the abuse. We need to be so disgusted by it.
Films with this type of hideous content must be shown
everywhere. I do not believe that someone will emulate or
replicate such a scenario. There is always a way to trigger
repulsion.

It's beyond comprehension what a human being is capable of
enduring. This enduring torture, in turn becomes a mechanism
of self-defence, further developed to either sustain a path to
misfortunes with a head straight or a mechanism of revenge that
turns a human body into a monster.

To say that because of a reassuring act of self-defence and a
series of abuse, it's normal to become normal, but of course, in
no way I would support such a behaviour. Pity, yes and great
pity towards the victim. More than ever there is a desperate
need to see the signs of abuse when it starts and even before it
begins. After it has happened, it's too late to change what has
been done.

A killer kill for a reason, just like a violent person or rapist. It is
either an act of revenge from something or someone about a
trauma endured, mainly in the past that a killer must carry this
trauma for life.

It is a high order, a survival order. In a war, it is a supreme
order, the soldiers were following orders and often on heavy
drugs, abdicating all responsibilities. This makes killing such an
easy mechanism to follow and process like a mundane habit, a
necessary routine of no consequence.

Chapter Four: The Making of T.

I never wanted to wait years trying to find the funding for a film,
so I just went along with the production, find a team willing to
help me. I had a top ten City advisor as a producer who also
spent 15 years directing and producing programmes for the
BBC, a director of Photography who won an Oscar, an Emmy
and several Baftas and plenty of people willing to provide a
voice but not act. I had the director of photography's film studio
in London Battersea, and a brilliant team around me. I studied
acting in the nineties and not in order to become an actor but to
direct and communicate so it did seem a most challenging job. I
have performed, rather than acted the role of G, Roosevelt and
DOC and have asked others to provide the voices.

Being very fond of whatever is reversed, like black and white or
white reversed, I use this "setting" (filter). I use animal masks.
Animal faces ...

I played each role, each interview, one interviewing the other
character.

The whole presentation gave it an air of being animated.

We used transition, albeit created one, a journey over Brooklyn
bridge in New York, a recurring theme, to mark the interview
and chapters.

One chapter consists of 45 minutes of email exchanges with the
voices of the protagonists, a chapter extremely vital to the
understanding of the story since one of the key murders occurs
during this exchange. A game is being played and fought and

the viewer is invited to play and be part of the interactions.

Many viewers complained that the key characters wearing "animal" masks are too deranging, preferring to be closely identified with a human protagonist. The catchphrase provided by most doctors -for people suffering with tinnitus- is: "just get on with it, ignore it and change your lifestyle". Not a long-term solution for a time bomb waiting to explode. It is not regarded as a disease or even a mental condition or an illness and yet this condition can easily paralyze the brain if not taken under control. Many people became addicted to painkillers and sleeping tablets as a result. It is not uncommon to witness people rolling on the floor in agony as the noise becomes deafening and insufferable. In this case many doctors might suspect drug abuse or some mental illness.

Humans are a machine and if this machine is invaded and controlled by some unknown forces; noises, ghosts or otherwise the consequences can be devastating for the sufferer but also for anyone else in close contact.

An analogy to too much reality in a film: Many viewers complained that the "weird" background music (some kind of brass and horns mix) is too deranging. The noise is one of the sounds of Tinnitus, the sound that Tinnitus sufferers often hear. Some viewers would have preferred instead the traditional sounds of explosions and loud music normally heard in films.

The white background symbolizes utopia: a land that is not supposed to be there and conveys a story that is not supposed to exist.

Chapter Five: T: Ghosts in the Machine

CONTENTS

INTRO

ACT I: INTERVIEWS

A series of interviews conducted by the mysterious DOC with two of his patients inside the psychiatric unit at the University of Alabama have resurfaced on the web.

The image quality is lousy and only a snippet of each interview has been made available.

ACT II: EMAILS

1. **R_REPLIED** Emails exchanged between Mr Roosevelt and DOC.
2. **G_REPLIED** Emails exchanged between G and DOC.
3. **Gnat REPLIED** Emails sent by G to DOC but not replied.
4. **R_Not REPLIED** Emails sent by Mr Roosevelt to DOC but not replied.

ACT III: LIVE

1. **TV NEWS** Introducing the action where and when G
    meets Mr Roosevelt, now the current president of the
    United States, live on TV.
2. **HOSTAGE** G has taken the president as a hostage.
3. **OUTRO** G meets his destiny.
4. **Previously, at the CENTER** DOC's final report five
    years ago
5. G's Forbidden Thoughts

ACKNOWLEDGMENTS

It may not have been a work of fiction.

A thriller.

Summary

An interactive novel, murder, mystery thriller in 3 acts revolving around the number 6 and the letter T, both being the proton and neutron of the story.

Two men from very different backgrounds meet and discover that they are both guided by invisible ghosts and they are in fact two machines forced to live a life haunted by an incurable condition: "T" (tinnitus).

The story begins with 66 interviews between the two protagonists G and Roosevelt and their psychiatrist, DOC.

During the inauguration of the tallest building in town, one man is holding the President of the United States at gunpoint and together they will disappear for 66 minutes out of the eyes of the world where they will confront the ghosts in the machine.

Dramatis Personae

DOC: Psychiatrist, English in his thirties

G, Gordon Griffith: patient 2366 in his twenties

Gordon has been referred to the Medical Centre as he was living rough in the streets and has been diagnosed with suffering from schizophrenia, and dementia. He had many small stints in various jails.

R, Roosevelt: Patient 2166 and later President Roosevelt the Second in his forties.

An aspiring politician, Republican and eager to lead a normal life in spite of his overpowering condition in order to achieve his goals as one of the leaders of his party.

Male TV news anchor

Female TV news anchor

FBI agents

We always have a guardian angel in life. Someone somewhere watching above our head and deciding what's best for us and thus triggering the events that will occur in later life. It's a game some people play.

It's a game I play. I'm in heaven or hell on a cloud server if you like. I'm watching over several people on earth.

I play with them and guide them to their natural destiny.

Everyone has a destiny.

I do have one and this is beyond my or anyone's control.

<u>Act 1:</u> INTERVIEWS

A series of interviews conducted by the mysterious DOC with two of his patients inside the psychiatric unit at the University of Alabama have resurfaced on the web.

The image quality is lousy and only a snippet of each interview has been made available.

The transcript of this video file runs like this:

1. Patient 2166: ROOSEVELT

DOC Mr Roosevelt the third?

ROOSEVELT DOC? I don't even know your name.

DOC My name is not important. May I call you Mr Roosevelt?

ROOSEVELT If you wish. May I call you DOC?

DOC If you wish.

1. Patient 2366: G

DOC Gordon is it?

G G!

DOC G, is it?

G Have you got a name, DOC?

DOC You don't need it. You won't have to call me. I will always be around.

G Will you? You're all a mystery, DOC!

DOC I'm not important here, you are!

G Is this why you have no name?

DOC Call me DOC!

---

2. Patient 2166: ROOSEVELT

ROOSEVELT DOC, finally: I despair in this place.

DOC What seems to be the matter?

ROOSEVELT The matter? I'm driving insane! I can't stand anyone. I hate anyone. I lied to my wife about my condition and this in my brain is killing me.

DOC Condition?

ROOSEVELT T. I have T.

DOC You have T?

ROOSEVELT Yes. I think I always knew I had it. I'm really scared that it will kill me.

DOC It will if you let it

ROOSEVELT I know but it's moving fast

DOC Don't let it

ROOSEVELT I'm already insane

DOC I don't believe you are!

---

2. Patient 2366: G

DOC Is there anything you want to tell me today?

G No. Do you?

DOC You're the one who can tell me your story.

G My story, is it?

DOC Your story!

G A hard luck story. A story overpowered by noises, noises turning into voices that I don't understand.

DOC Voices or noises?

G Both

DOC You hear them?

G The noise is inside my head but it seems that it's coming through my ears.

DOC Like an engine?

G Yeah...

DOC Like water flowing?

G Yeah, man! You have it too?

DOC No. Is it painful?

G Fuck yes. It seems to control me. I can't do anything. If I have a headache, it lasts a day and I even roll on the floor.

DOC I see. You have T!

G T?

DOC T is a condition, not an illness.

G Like a disease

DOC No, a condition. T is for Tinnitus.

3. Patient 2366: G

DOC How are you today?

G Pretty fucked up!

DOC Same as before?

G Same! So I'm not insane DOC?

DOC No, you only have a condition

G Does it mean I have to leave the centre?

DOC Not just yet

G Good. I don't have anywhere else to go

---

3. Patient 2166: ROOSEVELT

DOC Mr Roosevelt: I hope you have everything you require from the centre.

ROOSEVELT Yes. Thank you. *#Falling **slowly asleep***

DOC Is this a bad time Mr Roosevelt?

ROOSEVELT Yes. I'm feeling extremely tired. I was unable to sleep last night and I couldn't receive any sleeping pills.

DOC My apologies for this: we are trying not to medicate whilst there is still an on-going assessment.

4. Patient 2166: ROOSEVELT

DOC How is it? How does it really manifest itself inside?

ROOSEVELT It's hard to explain, it's like this. One day, you discover that you're born in a certain way. You almost believe that you've been possessed.

4. Patient 2366: G

G Feeling like you've been possessed. You're hearing noises and things and then you start to believe that someone is there.

5. Patient 2166: ROOSEVELT

ROOSEVELT Overwhelming... A sense of being possessed, a sense of loss even... Something is there and is about to take over yourself...

5. Patient 2366: G

G That thing... It gets you right inside the head; it echoes and
stuff. It's powerful. It drives you everywhere you go; it is ruling
your life.

6. Patient 2166: ROOSEVELT

ROOSEVELT It is a ghost that has access to your brain. This
thing is in control of your head and sometimes its noise is so
deafening, you have no idea how you are going to get through
the day.

6. Patient 2366: G

G It's killing me most of the time. It pushes me to do things. All
the fuckers around who did this to you. You hate everyone
around you. Someone did this shit to you.

7. Patient 2166: ROOSEVELT

ROOSEVELT No one seems to know how it got there; the noise is omnipresent. It used to be sporadic but now it's a whole power station with people guiding you day and night.

7. Patient 2366: G

G Someone did it to me. Sure. Someone is responsible for this shit and all the shit in the world. Someone, one day will pay for it.

8. Patient 2166: ROOSEVELT

ROOSEVELT And the doctors! There was only one who believed me, the one who knew... They always say that you have "to get on with it". "It will go away..." But you don't believe that, it's here to stay. It's a condition; a disease, it exists and it has a name.

8. Patient 2366: G

G Then the noise becomes like voices, then you hear the voices and you follow the voices wherever they tell you to go.

9. Patient 2166: ROOSEVELT

ROOSEVELT Yeah... I'm the crazy one! It's never the guys triggering the stuff: it's you, only you! That thing is in you and you have to live with it. They call it: T. Tinnitus. It's a condition.

9. Patient 2366: G

G We'll see how I'll be in ten years' time! I might be completely fucked up... I'm fucked up now and the noise is killing me... The ghosts in the machine... The ghosts are running this big engine and they are telling me to do things.

10. Patient 2166: ROOSEVELT

ROOSEVELT They call it: Tinnitus. The one that has caught this condition has to handle it alone. It's self-help. I got to ignore it. Some will succeed and some won't. I can't let that thing possess me. I need to get a grip; I've just been selected to be a candidate in my party... I may be running for Congress soon... No one will ever know. No one will ever need to know...

10. Patient 2366: G

G Hi DOC! Got any pills? I don't smoke. Can't smoke as you know so it seems fair enough? Jesus if I was smoking the smoke will torture T then I'll get even more tortured in return.

DOC I can't prescribe any medication for your condition.

G What have you got for me DOC?

DOC I'm here for you

G Where?

DOC Here!

G How can you fucking be here when you're not there?

DOC Please don't swear at me!

G What the fuck?

DOC I'm here to help you but I can't and I won't help you if you start howling abuses at me.

G Touchy man!

---

11. Patient 2366: G

DOC You can trust me, G.

G Trust you DOC? How the fuck can I trust you, man?

DOC I'm your psychiatrist!

G DOC: You're human! I wouldn't trust any human. PERIOD. Humans are so stupid! They are designed that way.

DOC I see, am I stupid?

G All humans have failings. They fail. It's imperfect: they are imperfect and uncontrollable.

DOC Uncontrollable?

G Uncontrollable!

DOC Animals?

G Most of them tend to behave far better. They have discipline. They don't have choices: they don't have a choice PERIOD. It's only one way for them.

---

11. Patient 2166: ROOSEVELT

ROOSEVELT Doc. You're not very bright, are you?

DOC I beg your pardon?

ROOSEVELT I hope you're really sorry for this, Sir.

DOC Sorry for what?

ROOSEVELT Never mind! I've sussed you out from the first interview and here we are 11 interviews later and you haven't sussed me out.

DOC I'm not here for this.

ROOSEVELT What are you here for?

DOC I'm here to help you; to control your fears and anxieties and to help overcome your condition.

ROOSEVELT Well, hurry will you DOC? Because so far T is winning.

12. Patient 2366: G

DOC G!

G DOC!

DOC What's up?

G What's fucking it up you mean?

DOC What's happening?

G *#Eyes wide shut, both hands over his head*

DOC G?

G *#Screaming*

DOC! Yes Doc! DOC, DOC, DOC! It's fucking killing me and they are telling me this. and ...

DOC "They"?

G Or "he" is. Fuck this! It's T. Always T!

#G fell off from his chair and is currently kneeling on the floor

DOC G!

DOC G *#Getting hold of G and lifting G and helping him walk out of the room whilst G is screaming blue murder in desperate agony*

12. Patient 2166: ROOSEVELT

DOC Mr Roosevelt

ROOSEVELT …

DOC Mr Roosevelt?

ROOSEVELT *#Squeezing his head using both hands*

DOC Mr Roosevelt?

ROOSEVELT …

DOC Mr Roosevelt?

ROOSEVELT Stop calling my name! Stop calling me all the time! Just stop calling me. I'm not here. Not anywhere. *#He gets up abruptly and rushes out of the room*

13. Patient 2366: G

DOC How do you connect with friends?

G I hate people and everyone hates me.

DOC And your friends?

G I have no friends!

DOC Why not?

G I hate people!

DOC Even where you are?

G I don't live anywhere. I hate anywhere and I'm homeless.

DOC Oh, yes. I remember. Sorry about that.

G Correction. I'm living here at the moment.

DOC Yes, that is true!

---

13. Patient 2166: ROOSEVELT

DOC Do you feel lonely at times?

ROOSEVELT I would be, I'm always alone.

DOC Is it painful?

ROOSEVELT Not as much as being with someone.

DOC Is it painful for you to be with someone?

ROOSEVELT Hell! I hate everyone.

DOC Where is this hate coming from?

ROOSEVELT I Have T! I can't respond to someone, not at the

same time. It all depends how I feel at the time, if someone is talking to me. I can't do anything. Just can't.

---

14. Patient 2366: G

DOC Do you have sex?

G Do you?

DOC I'm asking you!

G Sometimes.

DOC You haven't got a girlfriend. Have you?

G No.

DOC How do you meet someone, anyone?

G I don't. I haven't met anyone. Don't need anyone.

DOC I see...

G Do you?

DOC ...

G Do you really, DOC?

DOC Yes!

14. Patient 2166: ROOSEVELT

DOC How was your day so far?

ROOSEVELT T?

DOC Yes!

ROOSEVELT Like the sound of air flowing in the summer.

DOC In the summer?

ROOSEVELT Late evening!

DOC Bearable?

ROOSEVELT Almost.

15. Patient 2166: ROOSEVELT

ROOSEVELT *#Roosevelt keeps on staring at DOC for a few seconds then closes his eyes then starts the same process again. DOC is enjoying a perfect day and his enthusiasm transpires throughout the interview and this situation is upsetting Roosevelt*

DOC A good morning to you Mr Roosevelt!

ROOSEVELT ....

DOC That bad, is it?

ROOSEVELT ...

DOC How are you coping here so far Mr Roosevelt?

ROOSEVELT ...

DOC You look like you had a hangover!

ROOSEVELT I don't drink and this is a hospital.

DOC Yes, of course.

ROOSEVELT You're failing, DOC. You really are!

DOC   ...

---

15. Patient 2366: G

DOC How are you Sir?

G Sir? Am I?

DOC Sir!

G Well, I haven't killed anyone yet. It's been a while since the last time.

DOC The last time since...

G Since I've killed someone!

DOC You... have killed someone?

G I kill people, yeah. Fuckers mainly!

DOC Kill?

G Yeah, DOC. With a gun! Wanna be killed?

DOC ...

G Scared?

DOC I'll ignore that last remark.

G What: "scared"?

DOC No. The question before.

G Oh: "wanna be killed?"

DOC ...

G Scared then?

DOC ...

#A momentary break obstructed the interview only restarted by G

G And?

DOC *#DOC is taking a deep breath*

DOC I'll ignore this!

16. Patient 2166: ROOSEVELT

DOC Do you scream?

ROOSEVELT Scream?

DOC Yes, shout at people?

ROOSEVELT No, never at people. Only to myself.

DOC At Yourself?

ROOSEVELT In the air, in the park or by the sea: it helps!

DOC I see...

16. Patient 2366: G

G *#G is shaking his head.* Fuck this! They're banging against metallic tubes.

DOC T?

G *#Shouting.* Yeah. Fuck, fuck! And water is flowing with mega fireworks on top.

DOC Stop shouting, G!

G   #*Shouting even louder than before* Fuck you!

DOC Stop swearing at me!

G   #*Lowering his voice* I'm not swearing at you DOC, I'm just screaming

DOC Don't scream!

G It's my right to scream and shout!

DOC Do it in the park, G!

G I will. Bye DOC! #*G rushes out of the interview room.*

---

17. Patient 2366: G

G   I'm not the man you think I am, DOC!

DOC And who might you be then, G?

G   Might? What's that?

DOC May ... be. Forget it! Who are you, G?

G   Someone who's wished you'd never met

DOC I'd never wished I'd never met you. It was a pure coincidence that we've met, G!

G Not that pure. People who meet are always destined to meet. But if you knew who I was before I'd met you, you wouldn't have wanted to know me.

DOC I'm not sure how to respond since I didn't even know you before I did.

G *#G offers DOC his proverbial victorious "victory" smile*

DOC *#DOC responds by biting his lips staring at G and G staring at DOC*

---

17. Patient 2166: ROOSEVELT

ROOSEVELT Do you believe I can be cured, DOC?

DOC Mr Roosevelt: one can only get cured from a disease, an illness or an injury. Not a condition.

ROOSEVELT Will I improve my condition?

DOC It's entirely up to you. I can help you to get on with it but you're the only one who can control T.

---

18. Patient 2166: ROOSEVELT

DOC Mr Roosevelt?

ROOSEVELT *#Yawns*

DOC Tired?

ROOSEVELT Hmm...

DOC T?

ROOSEVELT I drank some filter coffee from the canteen. It's always boiling hot.

DOC I'm sorry

ROOSEVELT Yeah and then I always pour some cold milk inside to cool it off

DOC Not a good idea: cold and boiling hot never mix

ROOSEVELT Too right! I got a splitting headache since this morning

DOC Is it triggering T?

ROOSEVELT Not yet. It has to go away before it does collude with T *#Yawning away*

DOC It can't be long now

ROOSEVELT Why is coffee always so lousy these days wherever you go? Too hot, too bitter or too this and that. Too much detergent inside too!

DOC Detergent?

ROOSEVELT Yeah. After cleaning the machine, they rarely ever rinse anything: it never fails.

DOC Coffee never helps anyway and especially with T.

ROOSEVELT *#Yawns*

18. Patient 2366: G

G DOC the tea is really crap in here. You need 3 tea bags to make it OK.

DOC 3 tea bags?

G Yeah, man

DOC G, you must avoid caffeine: that's tea and coffee. It doesn't blend with T.

G I know but I can't feel sleepy all day.

DOC Eat oat cakes!

G Oat cakes?

DOC Oats, porridge!

G What am I, a horse?

DOC No, G...

G Thanks, DOC!

---

19. Patient 2166: ROOSEVELT

DOC If you really want to get out of here and get on with your life, you will really have to start to get a move on.

ROOSEVELT Really, DOC? Really? Moving on? Moving on to become this man living with T if I choose to be.

DOC If you choose to be so then you will choose to live!

ROOSEVELT To be or not to be. That is the question...

DOC It is my question.

ROOSEVELT I've spent most of my childhood trying to commit suicide and failed, so past adulthood, it's pretty clear that I'm destined to live.

DOC Glad to hear it

ROOSEVELT How does it go again: whether 'tis is nobler in the mind to suffer, the slings and arrows of outrageous fortune and who would bear the scorns of life... What's the rest?

DOC I'm not sure

ROOSEVELT Isn't Shakespeare English like you, DOC?

DOC Yes but not from the same century

---

19. Patient 2366: G

DOC Are you with me today?

G I can hardly be anywhere else. Can I?

DOC Again *#Raising his voice slightly, are* you with me today?

G If it means that you will stop shouting at me then yes. I'm with you.

DOC I didn't shout but merely raised my voice.

G It didn't sounded like this, DOC

DOC It wouldn't: your ears' canals are filled to capacity.

G You can say that again, DOC!

DOC Repeat what I've said?

G No. I meant yes, I agree with you

DOC Good. Glad to hear it!

---

20. Patient 2166: ROOSEVELT

DOC In order for me to help you, you will need to help me. I need you to describe your condition to me.

ROOSEVELT I thought I have been doing this for the last 20 days. Obviously, I was wrong…

DOC You have tried but you need to try harder!

ROOSEVELT Harder? It's like another echo inside my head...

DOC Echo? What echo?

ROOSEVELT The echo that reverberates inside my head. It comes and it goes.

DOC An echo of what?

ROOSEVELT An echo of whatever has been said before... It lingers on.

---

20. Patient 2366: G

DOC So, G...

G DOC?

DOC Tell me...

G Yes DOC?

DOC Have you ever had an echo blasting inside your head? Or several echoes?

G A few...

DOC A few from where?

G From nowhere, from things that have been said before

DOC Does the echo linger?

G Sometimes...

DOC *#Stares at G for 66 seconds*

G #G returns the stare for another 66 seconds and an echo seems to reverberate inside two heads

---

21. Patient 2166: ROOSEVELT

DOC I would like to know more about the sounds that you're hearing

ROOSEVELT All the natural elements combined DOC! Wind, fire, water and air.

DOC All at the same time?

ROOSEVELT Sometimes and sometimes the sound is just a whole forest burning. "Just": this word seems like luxury.

DOC You can still work, can't you?

ROOSEVELT If you can stand the heat, yes DOC!

DOC Does it get very hot?

ROOSEVELT It was a joke DOC. It's the sound NOT the actual heat!

21. Patient 2366: G

DOC I'd like to know more about the sounds you're hearing G.

G I can hear you DOC!

DOC And apart from me?

G At the moment it's the sound of water flowing

DOC Air?

G *#Raising his voice* Air!

DOC What does air sound like?

G Air sounds like air, DOC! You and I both know what chocolate tastes like because we've tasted it before.

DOC I have never experienced this before

G Well, it's like between water flowing inside a deep forest and the sound of electricity.

DOC The sound of electricity?

G You've never lived in DOC, have you?

22. Patient 2366: G

DOC You've mentioned yesterday about the sound of electricity. I'm a bit puzzled by this.

G Yes *#Mimicking DOC's accent and way of speaking* You would DOC! The sound of electricity is like the sound of a plane heard from a distance. From far away. Except that the volume is much higher.

You're very electric yourself DOC! What are you trying to discharge on me? Are you hitting on me?

DOC *#Staring at G in disbelief*

G DOC?

DOC Are there any other sounds that you can distinguish?

G Not right now, no.

22. Patient 2166: ROOSEVELT

DOC Will you ever tell your girlfriend about T?

ROOSEVELT When we will get married but I don't really believe so. She wouldn't understand. No one understands it.

DOC She might do

ROOSEVELT She might but at the same time it would make the suffering worse.

DOC Why is that?

ROOSEVELT If I keep T for myself then it becomes my own demon. It is anyway. It's my own personal struggle. If I don't want people to treat me differently then it's best to keep it private. Besides, what good would it bring to me? People would make allowances for me and feel sorry for me, for my behaviour. This in turn will never make me accepted as one of their equal. If I hide T, it will force me to fight T even more and help me to ignore it. If my surroundings know about T, they'll only allow T to develop and this will only be the death of me.

---

23. Patient 2366: G

DOC How was it when you have been sleeping rough in the streets?

G Rough!

DOC Bearable?

G When it wasn't freezing, when people like you didn't come around kicking us in the middle of the night with their feet or beating the hell out of us with baseball bats.

DOC Drunk people?

G Drunk or not, it's just something that they do for fun or because we exist: they fear a hobo. Tramp to you DOC!

DOC Fear?

G Fear that they might become like us. Kicking is bearable. A hard beating is felt months afterwards but it's still better than fire.

DOC Fire?

G They set fire on people sleeping on the streets. You didn't know that DOC?

DOC They set people on fire?

G Yes, DOC! All the time!

DOC Do they survive?

G Never! They burn to death. Yes, DOC! To death! Who's gonna call the fire brigade in the middle of the night? A passer-by who had already run away scared to death or another hobo skulking petrified in a corner somewhere with his imaginary iPhone?

DOC ....

---

23. Patient 2166: ROOSEVELT

DOC Do you know anyone else with T?

ROOSEVELT No

DOC Met anyone with T?

ROOSEVELT No

DOC Would you like to meet anyone else with T?

ROOSEVELT No

DOC: But you do want to meet people in general?

ROOSEVELT I don't have a choice. I have to meet people. I have to talk to people; I'm trying to be a politician.

DOC You don't like it?

ROOSEVELT No. It's torture. Having the sound of an engine inside whilst someone is talking to you about things that you can't understand because of the noise and couldn't understand anyway because it's too far out and stupid anyway.

DOC Do you hate people?

ROOSEVELT I don't hate anyone. How can I hate someone I don't even know? I just don't like anyone.

---

24. Patient 2166: ROOSEVELT

DOC Do you remember?

ROOSEVELT Yeah

DOC Remember things from a long time ago?

ROOSEVELT Yeah... sure. Anything

DOC Anything?

ROOSEVELT Anything since I was born. Every single detail. I remember it all the time. That's how I get through things. Remembering how things were before. Before T if such a life even existed.

DOC How do you remember?

ROOSEVELT By thinking about it, DOC!

DOC Yes, but what do you remember?

ROOSEVELT I can't share this with you!

DOC Why not?

ROOSEVELT It's private

DOC I'm your psychiatrist

ROOSEVELT I remember things to help myself. If what I remember becomes someone else's remembrance, it will cease to be mine.

DOC ?

---

24. Patient 2366: G

DOC You said once that you remembered the taste of things?

G Yeah?

DOC What else do you remember?

G I remember everything, everything since I was born

DOC Such as?

G Everything. I can't tell you. I'll lose my memory if I do.

DOC Lose it?

G Completely!

DOC Completely?

G Remembering is how I got through life. Trying to remember if things were better before. I'm already fucked up enough without losing my memory.

---

25. Patient 2366: G

DOC G, I've noticed you don't eat much at the centre?

G No. I don't have a food problem.

DOC You could have one if you don't eat

G I only eat a small amount. That's enough. I drink water when it's available.

DOC Do you sleep well?

G Alright I guess. Some nights I do sleep and some nights I don't.

DOC Some nights you don't sleep at all?

G Look here DOC. I sleep enough to stand up otherwise I wouldn't be able to stand on. I don't want to over-eat otherwise I wouldn't be able to walk or breathe. At least in this way, I'm still standing. Just in case.

DOC Just in case?

G Just in case I need to, I decide to end my life.

---

25. Patient 2166: ROOSEVELT

DOC Are you eating enough Mr Roosevelt?

ROOSEVELT Plenty, thank you DOC!

DOC You never overeat, do you?

ROOSEVELT No

DOC Sleeping enough?

ROOSEVELT I never sleep enough. I have T and T keeps me awake all night. Besides I'm a politician; my schedule is overloaded. It's 24/7 DOC!

DOC You're not working at the moment, are you?

ROOSEVELT No. I'm here. But I feel it is soon time for me to leave and re-join the real world.

---

26. Patient 2366: G

DOC How do you eat G? Do you cook?

G Not in the streets, DOC! No!

DOC Where do you go?

G I check the leftovers over a garbage pile or go to Starbucks.

DOC Starbucks?

G Starbucks! Yeah, man

DOC Isn't Starbucks expensive?

G No. Free

DOC Free?

G Free. All free! Everyone leaves their food on the table half eaten or not eaten at all. Coffee, hot chocolate, cakes, muffins. Muffins and cakes have too much sugar there and taste a bit like cardboard. I should know. When I can't sleep at night I chew and often eat the cardboard I'm sleeping on. Nearly a whole sandwich with smoked salmon inside, DOC! What's wrong with people, DOC? And on brown bread: your kind of food DOC!

DOC That's what people are leaving behind?

G Yeah. The food is not that bad. Better than at McDonald's and at Mc Donald's no one leaves the food behind.

DOC Every day?

G Every day, every hour

DOC You could catch some serious infections there, G!

G No. No problems people are leaving behind their fruit salads - half eaten or unopened- orange juices and often unopened. That's Vitamin C DOC! That's good for ya!

DOC Why do people leave food behind?

G They don't really go to eat at Starbucks. They go for a bit of coffee; they meet people and they go or they just buy something to use the toilets.

DOC I don't really go there but is anyone seeing you eating the food?

G No I don't know and I don't care. It's food gone to waste.

DOC Do you stay there?

G Yeah. To digest. I don't know what's inside the food but generally everything comes out after a while so it's wise to stay near the toilets. Starbucks has the best public toilets around. And it's free! The room is large enough to have a whole wash there. Not to bathe. Just wash. Plenty of tissues and a turbo drying. A fast dry. I strip, wash and turbo dry myself like that.

DOC *#Bewildered,* I'm not sure I want to go there.

G That depends if you want to eat inside or nearby a public toilet DOC

DOC …

---

26. Patient 2166: ROOSEVELT

DOC What kind of food do you eat?

ROOSEVELT I don't really eat much.

DOC Cakes, sweets?

ROOSEVELT No never

DOC Do you go out to eat?

ROOSEVELT Never. The food is always lousy and unhygienic.
So, there is no point and you always have to be nice to people
and still pay for it. It's lazy to eat out. I never do. I never have the
time anyway. I work all the hours of the day.

DOC Do you cook?

ROOSEVELT Basic stuff. My girlfriend cooks too but basic stuff
too.

DOC So Mr Roosevelt... What have you been doing in the centre so far? How do you spend most of your time?

ROOSEVELT Reading mainly. I had a lot of catching up to do.

DOC Reading?

ROOSEVELT Law books mainly. Capitol Hill has a lot of rules and regulations. One cannot step off the mark that easily.

DOC Step off?

ROOSEVELT Well. One has to blend in. There isn't a lot to know about being a politician, but the little there is to know one must ensure fluency and never cross any line.

DOC Does reading hurt?

ROOSEVELT Reading politics always hurts, DOC! T makes it even harder but I do not have a choice.

27. Patient 2366: G

DOC G...

G DOC?

DOC How do you occupy your days at the centre?

G I'm catching up on my sleep, DOC. I have a bed and regular meals here. Thanks!

DOC Watch some TV?

G Rarely: sometimes but never for long. It hurts too much with T. I have long walks in the park and every day I meet a weird DOC who always looks very queerly at me.

DOC *#Smiles*

28. Patient 2366: G

DOC What is it G?

G *#Staring at DOC in silence*

DOC G?

G *#Staring at DOC more menacing each passing second* I'm not feeling very comfortable right now.

#Anger and rage combined together seems to be brewing over G's face

DOC G? *#Fear is suddenly visible over DOC's face* G?

G *#Red with anger*   ...

DOC *#DOC suddenly stands up and leaves the interview room very slowly and always staring at G*

---

28. Patient 2166: ROOSEVELT

ROOSEVELT I believe my time is up here, DOC!

DOC Do you believe so?

ROOSEVELT Yes I do

DOC Do you really believe so?

ROOSEVELT Yes!

DOC I thought you still had T

ROOSEVELT You know I have T. T will never leave me

DOC Are you ready to ignore T?

ROOSEVELT I believe so. I do not have a choice in this matter. I want to live.

29. Patient 2366: G

DOC I've seen you in the park this morning on the bench staring at the trees

G ...

DOC You can't watch the time go by, you know?

G Why not?

DOC Time will catch you up!

G What?

DOC You'll be old before you know it, if you do

G I will be dead soon so it might be best to die young than old.

---

29. Patient 2166: ROOSEVELT

ROOSEVELT I have mentioned this before: I'm no longer comfortable being here.

DOC Are you ready to leave?

ROOSEVELT Just about...

DOC When you're ready we'll both know it

ROOSEVELT I'm about ready

DOC Yes, very soon

ROOSEVELT I can't hold the time for ever

DOC No one can!

---

30. Patient 2366: G

#66 seconds shot

DOC G?

G *#Motionless staring at DOC*

DOC G?

G *#His eyes are fixing DOC's eyes*

DOC *#Raising his voice* G! *#Getting angrier and angrier* Listen G, we've been there before. I'm not sure why you are so angry about it but you make me feel extremely uncomfortable right now.

G *#Crucifying DOC with his eyes. His breath is getting gradually heavier*

DOC *DOC's face is transfigured with fear. By the 66th second the door to the interview room suddenly opens. Mr Roosevelt appears. DOC switches the focus of his eyes toward the door whilst G remains seated facing DOC.*

ROOSEVELT DOC! I'm very sorry to barge in: I really need to speak with you.

DOC #*DOC stands up and leaves the room, glancing back at G still in the same position but now facing an empty wall*

---

30. Patient 2166: Roosevelt

DOC Have you ever taken any drugs?

ROOSEVELT Yeah, sure: everyone has, DOC! This is America. But I haven't taken any for a long time, not even prescription drugs; your kind of drugs, DOC! They are drugs too!

---

31. Patient 2366: G

DOC G. Have you ever worked?

G Yeah, man. Some days I have worked

DOC Is there anything you would like to do?

G Resting in a cemetery?

DOC That's not work

G It is: it keeps people empowered. Someone has to put me there.

DOC True! Unless of course...

G Unless what?

DOC Unless you end up in a pauper's pit!

G What?

DOC A mass grave?

G Yeah, man. That's possible too

DOC Honestly, did you ever hold on to a job for a few months?

G Never

DOC Weeks?

G Yeah weeks maybe... I was working in a kitchen once but the sound of burning gas made it too impossible for me.

DOC The sound of gas?

G It flows, man. Just like an explosion

DOC Like T?

G T is like the sound of gas too but hearing it from the outside makes it worse. It's like multiple explosions. No one can survive this.

DOC Unless you choose to...

G Choose?

DOC Choose to ignore it

G I can't ignore T. T will never ignore me.

---

31. Patient 2166: ROOSEVELT

DOC Why are you looking at me so closely Mr Roosevelt?

ROOSEVELT *#Staring at DOC ...*

DOC Mr Roosevelt?

ROOSEVELT *#Still staring in a complete trance*

DOC *#Glancing back and forth between Mr Roosevelt and the door*

ROOSEVELT *#In deep trance staring at DOC*

DOC *#DOC is now staring fixedly at Mr Roosevelt*

DOC ROOSEVELT

#The action is taking place for 66 seconds. All eyes veered from one direction to another but always focused on each other's face. Eyebrows frowning on occasions, lips twitching slightly and munching jaws. Heads are always steady, not a word or a sound is let out from either. Some breathing is heard half way through running at a gentle pace.

G *#G shakes his head as a mean of a hello*

DOC Hi G! Can you talk this morning?

G *#Shakes his head sideways to signify a "no"*

DOC What's wrong?

G My head is exploding

DOC T?

G No: a migraine: it lasted since -well- 6 days ago now and God it hurts.

DOC Have you taken anything for it?

G Yeah but all the pills made the problem even worse. It has been going on for 6 days now!

DOC It can't be a migraine. It can't last 6 days, a day at the most. If it had lasted 6 days then you would have been dead or in a coma.

G Then I'm dead and I'm not presently talking to you. I knew I was dead... I have T. I just never realised that I was already dead! Thanks, DOC! So, this is what you call hell!

DOC ...

32. Patient 2166: ROOSEVELT

DOC Mr Roosevelt: you haven't said very much since you have been at the centre and since we started all the sessions. You will need to communicate more and relay what seems to dominate your thoughts.

ROOSEVELT I thought that "thoughts" were actually private. I never realised it wasn't. As a Doc, aren't you supposed to read me regardless if you can break through my thoughts...?

DOC No. I can't. You need to tell me...

ROOSEVELT How come I've managed to read you like a book before and you've never been able to read me? Anyway, my migraine has increased now. A lock has been placed over my thoughts. That's a problem with all the changes in the weather and all on the same day. A bad headache combined with T can be lethal, DOC!

33. Patient 2366: G

G *#G stands against the wall in the interview room, eyes wide shut*

DOC G?

G ....

DOC G?

G *#G bangs his head over the wall*

DOC *#DOC stands up and rushes over G to prevent him hurting himself*

G *#G falls over the floor, his whole body shaking and rolls over in all directions without saying anything*

DOC *#DOC is still standing up and observes G without really moving* G, can you hear me?

G *#G is still shaking and rolling over the floor*

DOC G: you have to ignore it. Ignore it!

DOC G *#G holds his head with both hands and tries to get up aided by DOC then leaves the interview room and leaving DOC behind completely flabbergasted by G's behaviour*

---

33. Patient 2166: ROOSEVELT

ROOSEVELT Good morning, DOC!

DOC And a good morning to you too Mr. Roosevelt. I'm glad to see some of my patients not behaving hysterically.

ROOSEVELT Well, I have been behaving hysterically; I just try not to show it

DOC You mean you are ignoring your condition?

ROOSEVELT You could say that yes

DOC Has T ever affected you so much that you needed to harm yourself in anyway or roll over the floor?

ROOSEVELT Yes but I don't believe I have or would harm myself

DOC Roll over the floor?

ROOSEVELT Yes. Many times. But in the end, you've got to control it otherwise it will be the end.

---

34. Patient 2366: G

G I have been wondering if I kill ya it will remove T

DOC And how may I ask will it kill T?

G If you're not here anymore, you wouldn't trigger T anymore. I might still be in hell but T would be dead

DOC T will never die

G T is human. All ghosts are humans, they are mortals, DOC!

DOC Ghosts are already dead. They are ghosts: just spirits…

G So, do you believe in spirits, DOC?

DOC No and I am not T!

G T is human and a ghost is just a reflection of a human and I believe it is your reflection inside me.

DOC I'm not very comfortable with this!

#DOC gets up and leaves the room. As DOC is about to open the door, G speaks

G Why are you so afraid of me? I'm the one in hell, not you. Why are you running away from me?

DOC *#DOC leaves the room slamming the door behind him*

---

34. Patient 2166: ROOSEVELT

DOC Do you have sex?

ROOSEVELT No. Not really. I've had sex before and I do have a future wife but I avoid it; I only go through the motions and I don't really miss it. With T getting involved, it's like doing it with and in front of a lot of people. It's really off-putting.

---

35. Patient 2366: G

DOC Do you feel numb at times with your ears?

G Sometimes, yeah

DOC Do you swallow to make it go away?

G Yeah...

DOC Was it like flying on a plane?

G A plane, man? I've never been on a plane before. I've never even left this town, DOC! I don't even know what this town is called.

---

35. Patient 2166: ROOSEVELT

DOC Your girlfriend never came to see you at the centre?

ROOSEVELT No, never and she never will

DOC Why not?

ROOSEVELT She doesn't know I'm here and doesn't know I have T and she will never know.

DOC What have you told her about being away for so long?

ROOSEVELT I lied

DOC Lied?

ROOSEVELT I had to cover somehow. Being a politician, I said I had to enrol in a college in New York and will be away for some time.

DOC She doesn't suspect anything?

ROOSEVELT No. I called and emailed her.

DOC I see

ROOSEVELT I won't stay long here, will I, DOC?

DOC *#There is no reply from DOC, just a polite smile.*

---

36. Patient 2366: G

DOC Do you have sex?

G Are you hitting on me again, DOC?

DOC No, G. I'm only asking!

G No. Only by myself and very rarely. I had some girlfriends before but T always got in the way. Sex is a private thing and if T gets in the way, it would be impossible.

---

36. Patient 2166: ROOSEVELT

DOC How was your first sound therapy session this morning?

ROOSEVELT A complete disaster

DOC A disaster?

ROOSEVELT Trying to fight fire with fire is not a very good idea

DOC It's an accepted treatment...

ROOSEVELT Blasting various sounds into your brain, through your ears for an hour? That multiplies T like there is no tomorrow!

DOC I'm sorry to hear that

ROOSEVELT Where are you getting all these miracle treatments from?

DOC *#Unable to respond. Forces a polite smile.*

---

37. Patient 2366: G

G *#G wriggles his shoulders clearly disapproving*

DOC Do you feel fear or hatred?

G Fear or hatred? No. I don't fear anything. I just don't like anyone or anything in particular but yeah, I hate some people and some places, sure.

DOC Has it always been like this?

G Always

DOC I see.

G And you?

DOC Me?

G Are you full of anger and hatred?

DOC My personal opinion is frankly irrelevant.

G I see...

---

37. Patient 2166: ROOSEVELT

DOC You never really liked anyone haven't you?

ROOSEVELT No. Not really

DOC Your girlfriend?

ROOSEVELT We get on

DOC Your parents?

ROOSEVELT No, not really. They died so many years ago now.

DOC Friends?

ROOSEVELT No. I don't trust anyone. People always tend to take advantage of me but I'm too busy, anyway.

38. Patient 2366: G

DOC *#DOC shuffles through a pile of documents. He has got a series of images to show to G* What does this image invoke in you?

G Invoke?

DOC Provoke...

G Provoke?

DOC *#Slightly annoyed* Provoke! What reactions does it bring?

G Bring?

DOC *#Exasperated:* What do you think of it?

G Err... a badly drawn elephant?

DOC G *#DOC turns the picture over and have a look at it and suddenly G bursts into a fit of laughter for 66 seconds*

#When G has stopped laughing, DOC is completely befuddled.

DOC What was so funny?

G You, DOC you are! We should really hook up when I leave the centre. We really should.

DOC ?

G And?

DOC I'm not allowed to make contact outside my medical duties.

G I thought I was neither medical nor clinical. I thought I didn't have a disease, only a condition. It's not contagious, DOC!

DOC No. It's not!

G So, how about it?

DOC *#Staring at G for 66 seconds*

G I see

---

38. Patient 2166: ROOSEVELT

DOC Do you laugh sometimes?

ROOSEVELT No

DOC Never?

ROOSEVELT Not that I can recall. No: I tell a lie. Once, a few years back I laughed at some woman at Starbucks because she wouldn't change the filter coffee.

DOC Change?

ROOSEVELT Do a fresh one

DOC And you laughed?

ROOSEVELT Yes. I laughed but not without a reason. It was a laugh generated by years of anger.

DOC Anger?

ROOSEVELT They only brew their coffee every 60 minutes and after 20 minutes it's generally a revolting bitter stew but they never get it. Greed I suppose and you taste it more if you drink it black.

DOC You can always go somewhere else

ROOSEVELT Starbucks is somewhere else. It's everywhere!

DOC What did they say after your laugh ended?

ROOSEVELT Nothing. They don't think over there: they have the same angry faces they normally have. Well, that was in England. In America the staff tends to be less angry.

DOC Do you fly a lot?

ROOSEVELT Not if I can help it. It certainly is not removing T.

DOC Did you feel better after laughing out loud?

ROOSEVELT For a while. Yes. Well about 66 minutes later I felt the migraine coming on then water flowing in excess: it lasted a good 66 minutes for the migraine then another 66 minutes for the water falling in excess to stop but only to be replaced by the sound of a plane flying at a low altitude.

DOC Your recollection of events is amazing.

ROOSEVELT Yes. I would be able to have a perfect recollection: I've lived every second of it and the whole episode is presently being reprocessed in my head. I can feel the migraine coming on for the next 66 minutes followed by the sound of water flowing for another 66 minutes. Thanks for this, DOC!

DOC *#Completely gob smacked by the sheer incredulity of the reply.*

DOC What do you think would alleviate the sounds in your head?

ROOSEVELT Nothing can reduce or remove the sound

DOC Have you tried anything at all?

ROOSEVELT Staying underwater makes it... well, different; soothing, but it's still there. The sounds have sunk in

DOC Sunk?

ROOSEVELT Melted in. It's different underwater, smoother but sometimes defined. That could also be because it's mingled with other sounds from the outside. It's different in high altitude: sometimes it really hurts. It's so piercing like the sound of a police siren in some states running continuously.

DOC *#Staring prosaically at R*

ROOSEVELT But in altitude the strangest thing is that I ignore it subconsciously for a moment in time and it has just disappeared for a short while. I don't know but it's no longer there. I wonder how it would be in space. I guess the actual departure into space would be painful.

DOC Were there any moments in time when T wasn't there?

G No. Only when I'm asleep.

DOC Have you ever tried to treat the problem?

G Like taking pain killers?

DOC Yes

G Yeah, but it didn't work. It helps a bit when there is a migraine, that's all.

DOC Anything else that you've tried?

G Oh yeah running

DOC Running?

G If I had enough sleep before I can run a bit

DOC Does running help?

G It makes it well, OK. But only for a short while. It's back on as soon as I stop and I never run for a long time.

DOC How long for?

G Twenty minutes at the most, then I walk again for an hour

40. Patient 2366: G

G #*G sits still in another apparent trance*

DOC #*After a few seconds DOC tries to engage with G*

G are you with me or somewhere else?

DOC G #*No answers from G still deep inside his trance. G stares at DOC, focusing on his eyes*

#*DOC returns the stare peering into G's eyes. A deep eye exchange continues for 66 seconds*

---

40. Patient 2166: ROOSEVELT

ROOSEVELT #*R sits still, motionless and silent staring at DOC for a few seconds.*

DOC #*A few seconds later DOC tries to intercept this eye fixation*

Mr Roosevelt, can you stop staring at me like this? You are making me nervous and very uncomfortable. Mr Roosevelt? Are you with me?

ROOSEVELT #*Roosevelt continues to stare at DOC for the next 66 seconds.*

DOC #*During the entire Roosevelt stare, DOC can only but return the stare.*

DOC G, you will have to start thinking about leaving the centre soon. Where are you going to live?

G I live here at the moment...

DOC Yes but you can't stay here forever

G Nice coffee here

DOC You shouldn't drink coffee or tea in your condition.

G My condition? Am I pregnant?

DOC My apologies: *with* your condition.

G Coffee and tea helps. It makes it worse, confuses and messes things up but it helps the time go by.

DOC On the short run, perhaps but on the long run?

G There isn't any long run. You know that, DOC!

DOC Where are you going to live, G?

G Any bed where you live?

DOC G, you know I'm only your psychiatrist at the centre. We won't see each other after you have left.

G Do you think so? Do you really think we won't meet anymore, DOC?

DOC We can correspond by email for a while but we won't physically meet again

G Do you really believe that we won't meet again? Physically, DOC?

DOC *#Staring at G for a few seconds and biting his lips in the process*

---

41. Patient 2166: ROOSEVELT

DOC Mr Roosevelt, have you got any plans after I've gone and you will leave the centre?

ROOSEVELT Yes. Achieving my goals as a politician. I want to and will become a senator.

DOC Do you really believe that you can achieve this?

ROOSEVELT Yes I do. I really do. I have no choice. I have to go on, to move on and I have to aim high. There is no other way for me if I really want to live. Survive more like it.

DOC *#Staring anxious and unsettled at Roosevelt for a few seconds*

DOC How do you remember?

ROOSEVELT I only remember because I have to.

DOC You have to?

ROOSEVELT I have to in order to get through the day.

DOC What happens if you couldn't remember?

ROOSEVELT Everything would end, I guess. I have to remember each end of each day; I have to remember what exactly I did during the day, then I remember the day before then the week before, the month before, the year before until I was born.

DOC Is there any special thought process?

ROOSEVELT Not exactly

DOC It's not random, is it?

ROOSEVELT No. Just an endless list, all listed in reversed order.

DOC You've mentioned to me before that remembering helps you to get through the day. How do you remember?

G I keep on remembering the things I did before

DOC In a specific order?

G I guess. One before the last thing I remember

DOC And do you remember everything?

G Everything, man! Everything since I was born. What I was drinking when I was six on a Sunday and where I slept 3 years ago on a Monday.

DOC Does it all come together in one piece?

G No. One thing after the other

DOC Do you remember something specifically?

G Only if I'm asked by you but then I generally blank everything in this case.

DOC Why do you remember a specific thing?

G I don't. It just comes. It is in connection with something that happens at the time. The moment in time and then I go back very far away.

DOC How do you know it really did happen?

G What happened?

DOC The things that you remembered?

G I remember them because I've lived it all so I know it really did happen.

---

43. Patient 2366: G

DOC G: I have been informed that you phoned your bank from the centre and they have complained that you have been abusive. You can't do this from the centre and it never helps to be abusive. I had no idea you had a bank account.

G *#Flummoxed* 'Scuse me? You have just been abusive to me and highly offensive and for this I would have to report you, DOC!

Firstly, I do have a small bank account. Most hobos do. Thanks for being so offensive.

Secondly, I was not offensive over the phone but any member of staff these days when they have their nervous breakdown will say that anything they don't understand is abuse.

Thirdly, how on earth did they know I was here? They may have done a call back but it would have meant a break in the patient's confidentiality to even acknowledge that I was here.

Lastly, I'm fully aware that I'm not directly paying for this useless treatment but a charitable organisation is and they can still sue the centre for this. I'm not that stupid DOC! Uneducated, yes. I don't believe we have anything to say anymore. DOC!

G DOC *#G leaves the interview room boiling with rage and slamming the door behind him leaving DOC completely aghast and shell shocked*

---

43. Patient 2166: ROOSEVELT

ROOSEVELT *#Roosevelt has just entered the interview room. He can barely stand up. He sits on the chair, gives a quick glance at DOC then falls asleep over the table*

DOC Mr Roosevelt? *#Patting Roosevelt left shoulder* Mr Roosevelt?

DOC *#DOC is completely flabbergasted. He cannot take in that Roosevelt fell asleep in front of him. Too insulted that one of his patients could have fallen asleep during one of his conversations, it has failed to occur to him that given Roosevelt's condition, he may not have been able to sleep the night before*

---

44. Patient 2166: ROOSEVELT

DOC Do you spend much time online?

ROOSEVELT Web?

DOC Yes

ROOSEVELT Not if I can help it. I have nothing to do there, nothing to look at and I don't know anyone

DOC Well you might meet someone online

ROOSEVELT Online? I didn't know you were that stupid, DOC!

DOC There is no need to insult me

ROOSEVELT You are! Sometimes I feel that you are completely stupid and ignorant.

DOC I'm still evil, am I?

ROOSEVELT You're the one triggering T

DOC How am I doing this?

ROOSEVELT You are forcing me to remember

DOC Remembering get you "through things" "through the day"

ROOSEVELT Yes, it does when I keep this inside me and not when it is disturbed and brought out on the outside. Inside me: it's a train of thought: outside and it's broken. Thanks DOC!

44. Patient 2366: G

DOC You're not very keen when it rains, are you?

G I do like the rain, I just don't like the weather when it changes. It always triggers a long-lasting migraine.

DOC And the sun?

G That's different: I love it when it's hot, it helps me to forget about T but I can never look at the sun or it will blind me. A few times when I was in high altitude in the mountains, the sun pierced through a window then through my head -it felt like it- it was like if someone had broken some glasses and all the pieces were entering inside. It lasted for 66 minutes followed by a long migraine. Sometimes there is an explosion during the migraine. I guess it's like the sound of a bomb exploding, that loud and that distinct, and then it generally is followed by a light humming then a few birds tweeting around.

45. Patient 2366: G

G *#G is getting more assertive, concise and belligerent with his replies*

DOC Do you still have a lot of trouble sleeping?

G When I sleep, I sleep. If I can't, during the next day, it's debilitating. I'm a walking zombie: I'm not really tired; I just can't function for several hours until I reach the point when I really can't stand up and then I collapse somehow, somewhere, anywhere.

DOC *#Following G's answer, DOC is stunned. A clear sign of anxiety is brewing over his face. DOC is clearly at a loss on how to interpret G's answer and how to respond*

---

45. Patient 2166: ROOSEVELT

DOC Do you feel you are now getting enough sleep?

ROOSEVELT I never get enough sleep, DOC! And I probably never will. As you know, there is someone else inside me who never sleeps!

46. Patient 2366: G #46 R: BLANK FILE

DOC *#DOC hasn't slept at all well the night before. He has pouches under his eyes. In fact he hasn't slept well in the past few weeks. He feels more and more helpless and vulnerable and this morning is no exception*

G, don't you find life in general a bit lonely?

G Lonely?

DOC You're not with anyone and don't really know anyone and have no family.

G No. I told you: I hate everyone -including you-.

DOC *#His eyes deepen*

G People are just parasites: they use people, abuse people, make a living out of people. Just like you: you make a living out of me.

DOC Am I abusing you?

G I'm not sure but you are making a living out of me, for sure.

DOC I would agree with you there

G And at the end of my time there you will end up either richer or still in employment whilst I'll end up in the streets. The payment you receive through me will still be yours. I helped you but you wouldn't help me when I leave.

DOC I'm trying to help you now and we can still communicate by email afterwards.

G Until when? Until you die?

DOC Perhaps not that long. My email system won't be working after a while as our sessions will still be limited in time.

G But will your email system last until you die?

DOC *#DOC is suddenly transfigured with fears. He doesn't know what to answer or if he has actually heard it correctly. He sits motionless for 66 seconds facing G*

G *#G returns the stare and they together share 66 seconds of terrifying thoughts*

46. Patient 2166: ROOSEVELT

DOC Are you using the web at all?

ROOSEVELT Only for emails. If I stare at a screen for too long,
TV or computer then T is back on at full blast

47. Patient 2166: ROOSEVELT

ROOSEVELT Hi DOC! You don't look so good. Got T?

DOC *#Dishevelled and unshaven*

ROOSEVELT I'm not sure if it is due to the treatment I've
received here but I can really say that T has increased
dramatically. It's now permanent; a continuous flow of noises.
The voices are inside too but I can't understand them. I'm
fighting it: fighting to ignore it, fighting T.

DOC *#DOC sinks in his chair, dissolute looking and falls asleep his
head and arms on the table leaving Roosevelt completely stunned*

47. Patient 2366: G

DOC *#It's nearly 50 days after DOC first interviewed G and Roosevelt and he is slowly turning into a shadow of himself. His eyes are blurry due to a lack of sleep dated back from several weeks now, there are deep furrows in his cheeks and he looks extremely emaciated. He is finding more and more difficult to comprehend his patients and for reasons unknown to him, fear seems to be omnipresent whenever he addresses G*

G Hey, DOC. You look tired again. Where have you been?

DOC *#Looking at G with extinct eyes*

G You may need to see a DOC, DOC! Or you may need to start a few serious sessions with me.

#That last remark from G made him shudder

DOC I'm fine G. Really, just overworked.

---

48. Patient 2166: ROOSEVELT

ROOSEVELT I hear there is a member of staff missing? I hope nothing serious, DOC?

DOC I'm not sure: a nurse has been reported missing for a week now. Who mentioned it to you?

ROOSEVELT One of the security guys. He even questioned me about it.

DOC: Well... They have to ask whoever has been in contact with the nurse for help. Nothing to worry about.

---

48. Patient 2366: G

DOC *#Eager not to appear tired and slow, DOC kick-starts the session*

Good morning, G!

G DOC!

DOC You seem to be controlling T much better now

G Better? No. T is presently more powerful and stronger than never. It's just that the humming sound in the background is less loud but the voices are getting clearer.

DOC What voices?

G The voices of T. They used to be more distant and now they are in the foreground.

DOC What are the voices saying?

G They decide things, telling me to do things

DOC What kind of things?

G Tell me to warn people

DOC Warn people?

G Anyone that T feels that they are getting in the way

DOC In the way...

G In T's way

DOC *#DOC shivers with extreme anxiety. Something is clearly occurring here but he is as yet unable to fathom what it is.*

---

49. Patient 2166: ROOSEVELT #Part1

ROOSEVELT DOC: a detective has asked me more questions about the missing staff member.

DOC More questions?

ROOSEVELT Yes. I've been officially questioned by the police. What is this? A murder inquiry now?

DOC *#That last sentence provoked a glare of horror on the face of DOC*

Surely no one has been murdered. It's unthinkable!

#The thought of a homicide seems to resonate inside DOC's mind. His confusion is still visible over his face for a few hours. DOC is facing another day unable to work or function correctly

G *#G is already seated in the interview room waiting for DOC who is slightly late. There seems to be 66 seconds wait until DOC finally makes an appearance*

G Hey, DOC! Late this morning?

DOC My apologies G. I have been questioned by the police about another missing member of staff. You might have heard about the problem? Have you been questioned by anyone?

G No. Not yet. Why should I be questioned?

DOC They are questioning everyone. It's routine.

G The police always get it wrong. They never question the right people.

DOC The right people?

G The murderer

DOC Murderer?

G I hear it was homicide...

DOC *#DOC is getting really confused here*

G Well, missing people are usually murdered, aren't they?

DOC I... suppose so

49. Patient 2166: ROOSEVELT #Part 2

ROOSEVELT Hey, DOC! Another missing person? What's going on? Surely the staff may have just quit the job?

DOC Well, they are looking into it

ROOSEVELT I wish they'd stop questioning me. They did it again this morning. For the first missing person, they believe it's homicide and someone local.

DOC Local? *#DOC seems to be again paralyzed by deep confusion, unable to comprehend what can be taking place here*

50. Patient 2166: ROOSEVELT

ROOSEVELT They have found the body of the missing nurse

DOC Have they?

ROOSEVELT Yes. Haven't you heard?

DOC No. I have had too much paperwork to catch up on and new patients to see.

ROOSEVELT She was found in the boiler room.

DOC The… the boiler room?

ROOSEVELT Yes. She was stabbed apparently but I don't have many details

DOC How awful!

ROOSEVELT It is. I suppose they will release more details soon. In the meantime, the hunt for the other missing girl is still on-going

DOC Yes but I thought she was one of the occupational therapists

ROOSEVELT The missing nurse?

DOC Yes. I meant the other missing person

---

50. Patient 2366: G #G's thoughts@End/2

DOC G. Is there anything more you wish to tell me?

G About what?

DOC About the voices you seem to be hearing. Are they saying anything?

G They are always saying something...

DOC About what you have to do?

G Yeah

DOC What have they told you to do lately?

G To teach someone a lesson

DOC A lesson?

G Someone who disrespected T

DOC *#Not sure he heard it correctly*

What did you say?

G I didn't say very much. Anyway, it's all over now!

DOC *#DOC is sensing something but cannot figure up what it is*

---

51. Patient 2166: ROOSEVELT

ROOSEVELT It's getting really unsettling here. There is a serial killer at large and rumours are flying high!

DOC Rumours?

ROOSEVELT Rumour has it that it's one of the patients from the centre

DOC Really?

ROOSEVELT But other rumours contradict this. They talk about a jealous boyfriend

DOC I see

DOC G!

G DOC!

DOC You're here early, I can see

G Yeah: you seem to see better than the others this morning

DOC The others?

G The cops! They are asking everyone questions since the
murders started but they never got around to question me

DOC Do you have anything to say to them?

G Well, you never know!

DOC *#DOC is very unsettled and moves about on his chair*

G You know cops: they are like psychiatrists, they are always
missing the point! *#Smiles at DOC*

DOC *#DOC is forcing a tiny smile. Visibly shaken. DOC doesn't
understand. G is somehow making jokes and it seems to be provoking
something but to what purpose, it's unclear to DOC.*

ROOSEVELT DOC!

DOC Mr Roosevelt!

ROOSEVELT About time too. I'm telling you; the situation is getting really unbearable now

DOC What's the matter?

ROOSEVELT What's the matter? They have found the body. It was a male nurse. His face was completely mutilated, possibly with a big kitchen knife from the centre's main kitchen.

DOC Oh my God!

ROOSEVELT Yep. They have found the body inside the swamps by the park

DOC Who would do a thing like that?

ROOSEVELT That's why they are investigating and that's why I have been questioned again this morning

DOC I'm very sorry about this

ROOSEVELT Have you been questioned?

DOC No yet, no!

DOC Good morning G!

G Yeah. Very nice day, I'm sure!

DOC What is the progress with your voices?

G The voices? They are still there; hundreds of them

DOC Hundreds?

G Yep and growing. At the moment they are having a major conference.

DOC A conference?

G Yeah. All of them yapping away. They need to reach some decisions.

DOC What decisions?

G They need to decide on my next move

DOC Your next move?

G Yeah. Somebody has to tell me.

DOC G *#They are both staring at each other for 66 seconds. Both motionless, without real expression on their faces trying to figure up one another*

G *#This morning G seems to be lost in his labyrinthine world of layers*

DOC Morning G!

G Hmm?

DOC Good morning, G!

G Hi, DOC!

DOC *#Very casual* Hearing any more voices?

G No. T is dinning in my head; a sort of vapid random scream. It's horrendous. There is a thumping sound or more like a bumping, sort of a heart beating for a few seconds then it stops for a few seconds then it starts again at regular intervals. Generally, my hearing is at its lowest when it happens and my ears' lobs are all blocked

DOC I'm so sorry...

G I bet you are. I have to leave now anyway. I'll be better off in the park. The noise is going up.

DOC Very well

DOC Mr Roosevelt, have the voices continued to call?

ROOSEVELT The voices are always calling me and talking to me. They are guiding me but I refuse to take any notice.

DOC Do you really feel that there are more than one voice calling?

ROOSEVELT Yes: it's the whole United Nations in there! They all argue and disagree at the same time.

DOC Can you distinguish them?

ROOSEVELT DOC if I start doing this I'll never be able to fight T! But yes. I can: so far I can count nearly 100; I stopped counting at 66 but there are many more but I stopped isolating them the day I decided to ignore T.

DOC How can you tell the amount of voices?

ROOSEVELT They always appear at some point, one by one. Always in definite layers from the Northern hemisphere to the Southern Hemisphere.

DOC And the voices couldn't have been just sounds?

ROOSEVELT No. Voices, real voices!

54. Patient 2366: G

G Oh, DOC!

DOC What is it G?

G There is that thumping sound again...

DOC I see

G You see? You don't see anything, DOC! You never see anything DOC! You don't even see what's coming to you. I'm only trying to protect you here.

DOC *#DOC was suddenly captured by a sort of spasm. G's last remark made him shudder. He is still unsure as to what exactly G is referring to*

G *#G is leaving the room*

54. Patient 2166: ROOSEVELT

DOC ROOSEVELT *#Mr Roosevelt is very late this morning: DOC was getting very impatient. Mr Roosevelt is rushing breathless into the interview room*

DOC Oh! Mr Roosevelt! I wondered what happened to you!

ROOSEVELT My apologies DOC. I have been questioned again by the Gestapo.

DOC I'm sorry?

ROOSEVELT The cops! They've questioned me about the new missing person

DOC #Bewildered Another one?

ROOSEVELT Yes, DOC. Another one!

DOC #Unable to respond. Has started scratching his beard

ROOSEVELT Look, DOC. I need to rush off to the bathroom. We're gonna have to postpone this interview, I'm sorry.

ROOSEVELT DOC #Mr Roosevelt leaves the interview room. DOC is left alone completely befuddled for 66 seconds. He cannot figure up what is happening

---

55. Patient 2166: ROOSEVELT

DOC #DOC is shuffling through his notes and scratching his beard every few seconds

ROOSEVELT Don't tell me you haven't heard, DOC?

DOC What happened now?

ROOSEVELT The whole centre is in a state of mayhem and it's in the outside world too: my girlfriend called me on my cell and mentioned briefly about the 3 murders at the centre. She doesn't know I'm here and I've very nearly dropped my foot in it.

DOC 3 murders?

ROOSEVELT Yeah, homicides. They have found the third missing nurse. A male nurse in his twenties: they had to drain the swamps last night. What world are you living in DOC? You seem completely oblivious of what is happening at the centre.

DOC I'm sorry. I have been rather preoccupied by some paperwork lately. 3 murders now...

ROOSEVELT Yeah. It sounds impossible; it brings everything into a clear perspective

DOC What does?

ROOSEVELT The murders!

DOC *#DOC is unable to see what Mr Roosevelt means*

ROOSEVELT *#Mr Roosevelt can see DOC's disarray*

The murders make you think about life and death, DOC. About life: wanting to fight T!

DOC Yes. Yes I suppose it does

G DOC *#G is late this morning and DOC is getting restless, scratching his beard more poignantly than usual*

DOC *#DOC has been very nervous and anxious of late and his face is somewhat dishevelled: even though his thick black beard that has been growing steadily since the murders started it is clearly visible around his eyes that he is completely worn out by too many sleepless nights.*

G Come on DOC. It's not going to work. You need to face up to things. You can't face death in this condition!

DOC Face death? *#His left hand started to tremor slightly*

G Yeah, DOC! 3 deaths already! It's not yet the end of the world!

DOC *#DOC is deeply shocked by the sheer scale of G's determination to face life again. The 3 murders seem to have re-invigorated him*

G DOC *#G displays an impromptu smile of victory and DOC is again completely paralyzed for 66 seconds, transfixed and unable to fathom whether or not something is going on here*

G Hey DOC! Another week like this and you will be able to use your beard as a towel.

DOC Yes. I'm sorry: I do need to shave, don't I? I just haven't found the time.

G It makes you look more intelligent

DOC *#Forcing a tiny smile*

Thank you

G You're welcome!

DOC So, G: have you received any more guidance lately?

G Guidance?

DOC From the voices?

G Yeah man, all the time. It's just that I don't always get what they are saying.

DOC How do you know what they are saying to be right and true?

G I know it's true when they tell me things. I know this because they are inside me. They are T. You can't be righter than T!

DOC Is T always right?

G T is always right. He knows everything. He knows right through you, DOC! *#Gives DOC a smile*

DOC *#DOC is forcing himself to return the smile*

---

56. Patient 2166: ROOSEVELT

DOC *#DOC is already inside the interview room waiting impatiently for Mr Roosevelt whilst shuffling his papers*

ROOSEVELT A new murder has been announced

DOC Another one? *#Both hands shaking followed by a convulsing tremor through his body*

ROOSEVELT Steady on, DOC. I'm not the murderer. But there is still a lunatic at large within the centre and if the cops can't find who it is, we could be next!

DOC Next?

ROOSEVELT Yes, DOC! Next!

DOC *#DOC's face is becoming all red and he started to sweat heavily*

ROOSEVELT DOC, are you all right?

DOC Err, yes. Will you excuse me? I need to go to the bathroom. Thank you.

#DOC gets up and storms out of the interview room

G 4 murders so far DOC!

DOC 4? Not 2?

G No, only 4. That's the final count

DOC "Only"? What do you mean? Were you expecting any more?

G Well, I thought there would be 6 murders in all. But it can still happen...

DOC 6?

G Yeah, man. T told me.

DOC *#DOC is again transfigured with fear. He moves his head backwards and vomits on the wall*

G Oh, man. What's the matter with you? Can't you face death like a man? Pull yourself together, DOC!

DOC *#DOC is unable to speak. He leaves the interview room in a jiffy*

57. Patient 2166: ROOSEVELT

ROOSEVELT There is a serial killer at large and I'm still a murder suspect. I really have enough. I couldn't even leave even if you'd allow me to.

DOC I'm really, really sorry about all this. I don't believe it will take any longer than a week. I myself have been questioned by the police this morning.

ROOSEVELT Surely you can't be a murder suspect?

DOC They treat anyone as a suspect. Anyone who may have been in close contact with the victims.

ROOSEVELT DOC *#All puzzled*

DOC God! *#Scratching his beard*

ROOSEVELT Yes!

58. Patient 2166: ROOSEVELT

ROOSEVELT Who do you think would have murdered the nurses?

DOC I have no idea

ROOSEVELT Not a clue?

DOC No. Look here on things: one thing is that the murders should not in any way affect your recovery.

ROOSEVELT It won't. Trust me. I'm more determined than ever to leave this place and succeed with my life. No serial killer will change this.

DOC Good. Very good. I'm very glad to hear this. Err...Thank you.

ROOSEVELT Yeah. Thank you, DOC!

ROOSEVELT DOC *#They both stand up and leave the interview room together. Mr Roosevelt invites DOC to leave first then follow soon after*

---

58. Patient 2366: G

G Hey, DOC! When are you going to shave this beard? I can see some mushrooms growing outside!

DOC I'm really sorry. I'm in the process. It has been a very difficult month.

G Difficult? A lot of work?

DOC Well, yes and the murders...

G Oh, yes. The murders. But the murders have been committed; gone. Why still bother with them?

DOC They are human beings and fellow staff members. I didn't know them personally but that isn't a reason. Besides, there is still a serial killer at large...

G Yes. At large! Does it bother you, DOC?

DOC Yes. I can be killed!

G Yes, DOC! You can be killed! But you haven't been killed yet, have you?

DOC Err... no

G So, don't worry about it. Enjoy life whilst you're still alive!

#G ends his sentence with his usual victory smile

DOC G *#This time DOC has a real problem in returning the smile. He breathes heavily. He is not able to take anything in. He is scratching his beard. After a few seconds of unbearable anxiety:*

G *#G breaks the silence*

I'm off, DOC! I've promised to help in the kitchen; some meat to chop.

#G leaves the interview room leaving DOC stranded and all alone agonising and sweating from all over in silence for 66 seconds

59. Patient 2366: G

G Hey DOC! You're looking worse and worse!

DOC Thanks, G!

G So...You're not dead, yet?

DOC What? *#Interrupted short by G*

G I'm not very happy here. I have a roof over my head and food every day for sure but it's what they're doing in the park that I can't stand!

DOC What are they doing in the park?

G Some mass killings, that's what!

DOC Mass killings?

G The killing of the trees! Cutting them, even removing the roots! There are some very old trees there!

DOC I suppose they have to re-organize things every now and then.

G Reorganise? This is a carnage! There was a small forest there and now it's a desert! One of the trees was at least 1000 years old! Is this how you treat old people at the centre? It was still full of life. Without trees we don't exist: we can't breathe. You should know this, you're a scientist!

DOC I'm a scientist, but not that kind of scientist.

G I always knew that you never knew very much, DOC!

DOC: Well... *#Cut off by G*

G I bet the president is responsible for this

DOC The president?

G The president of the United States! He should be hanged for high treason!

#The window was left ajar and a powerful wind stormed inside blowing all of DOC's paper on the floor. G is helping the DOC to tidy up the mess. The wind has vanished after a few seconds and DOC shuts the window. They both leave the room

---

59. Patient 2166: ROOSEVELT

ROOSEVELT I believe the biggest evil in this world is palm oil!

DOC Palm oil?

ROOSEVELT Yes. They are trying to kill everyone with it.

DOC How?

ROOSEVELT All food and cosmetics contain the stuff. It's cheap stuff. It renders people obese and it is proven to be carcinogenic. I thought you were a scientist; you should know these things!

DOC I'm not that kind of scientist. I'm a psychiatrist.

ROOSEVELT Well, DOC! If this isn't the work of a devil, I am.

DOC You?

ROOSEVELT Yep, I was born on the mark of the devil. On the 6th of January 1966 at 6 PM, 6 minutes and six seconds passed.

DOC That's a lot of six

ROOSEVELT Indeed, DOC! It could have been worse, though

DOC Worse?

ROOSEVELT Yes it could have been the 6th of June 1966: 666 then at 6 PM 6 minutes and six seconds.

DOC I suppose you're right. You may be saved there!
#Displaying a faint smile

ROOSEVELT I hope so. Numbers are a strange thing. Will you agree, DOC?

DOC Yes I suppose they are. They define us: they are our DNA

ROOSEVELT Thanks, DOC! You said I may be saved and yet you said that they define our DNA then I am the mark of the devil!

DOC Correction: you're not quite the devil: you weren't born with the number 666. In June that is. Besides you will still have "1" and "9" before the "66" in "1966". Therefore, I don't believe you qualify.

ROOSEVELT Thanks, DOC! That's a relief.

DOC You shouldn't read too much into these things and it's only a religious superstition. Nothing to worry about. You can trust me, I'm a doctor!

---

60. Patient 2166: ROOSEVELT

DOC *#After an extended weekend break, DOC has been transformed. He is all refreshed and re-energized. He is all clean shaven and even cut his hair. His hair was growing so fast they were about to outstretch the length of his beard*

DOC Hey. Mr Roosevelt!

ROOSEVELT Hey DOC! Is it really you? I don't recognize you: all cleaned up!

DOC I had time to rest...

ROOSEVELT You could now do with putting some weight on. How skinny are you?

DOC I have always been this way

ROOSEVELT Well as long as you're healthy. I'm neither overweight nor skinny myself but if I stop running, I'll put on all sorts of crap inside my body.

DOC Hi G!

G Hi DOC!

DOC G: you have been transformed somewhat since you first arrived at the centre. I'm glad you've managed to put some weight on: you were so skinny when you first arrived here!

G Look who's talking!

DOC Yes but I've always been like this

G So am I. It's easy to put on weight when you have regular meals. Food doesn't come that easily when you're sleeping rough in the streets but if you don't eat, you starve and you become skinny. Easy! Glad you shaved this beard off, DOC!

DOC Yes. G, tell me: are you still hearing voices?

G Yeah. The voices move and navigate between layers and layers of voices. It's a maze of voices and one of them, at some point rises above the others and dictates the way forward.

DOC Voices not sound?

G It's a sound when it's not speaking but when it does, it becomes a voice. In general, all sounds define something or someone and signify a message.

DOC A message?

G A call, a word or a meaning.

DOC *#DOC first impression of G was that of a broken homeless, hobo and a bit dumb. As the months went by he couldn't help thinking that beneath the surface hides an extremely intelligent man and perhaps too intelligent for his own good*

---

61. Patient 2366: G

G Another five days to go, G

DOC Have you sorted out a place to live yet?

G Yes, I have a DOC. The social services Lady from the centre fixed me something up.

DOC Any jobs lined up?

G Yeah. Apparently, I have to talk to the welfare office.

DOC As you know the organisation that paid for you to be at the centre won't be able to anymore. But you will be able to communicate with me by email. It won't be forever and the email address will be limited in time.

G Ok, DOC! Thanks. For how long?

DOC I'm not sure

G Is it up to me to decide?

DOC *#Confused: What* do you mean?

G Well. If you're not sure, maybe I do. Maybe T knows.

DOC Well, it certainly is up to T. How long T will manifest itself and how long you will be able to cope.

G I thought as much

DOC But as I have said, funds for this treatment are now limited

G I guess I will have to hang on then, DOC!

DOC *#More confused* Yes

---

61. Patient 2166: ROOSEVELT

ROOSEVELT Hi, DOC!

DOC Mr Roosevelt, you seem to be in excellent shape and all radiant as well.

ROOSEVELT Thanks, DOC! I seem to be.

DOC As I have mentioned before, your treatment will end in 5 days -well another four days after today- and after this we won't see each other anymore.

ROOSEVELT Never?

DOC No. I don't believe so. I have been as far as I could with you. We will be able to communicate by email for a while. So, if there is anything with T, you will be able to let me know.

ROOSEVELT Thanks, DOC. It's unbelievable: there have been

61 interviews already. I'm not sure if I will recognize the world anymore.

DOC I'm sure you will

ROOSEVELT I will be marrying my girlfriend this month. We've decided on that.

DOC I'm very glad to hear it

---

62. Patient 2166: ROOSEVELT

ROOSEVELT I have to say, DOC, that at present I can only hear a mild air-conditioning system. It has been the case for a while.

DOC I'm glad to hear it

ROOSEVELT Obviously, there are things that I need to avoid and things that I need to do.

DOC How will you cope if you are asked many questions by various people or hold any conferences?

ROOSEVELT The same as I have done so far with you, DOC! Holding on!

DOC Is this what you have been doing here then?

ROOSEVELT Yep

DOC I thought T went away

ROOSEVELT T will never go away. But I can ignore it. I can
communicate with you, talk to you and still ignore it. I can
ignore it now better than I ever did.

DOC I'm glad to hear it, Mr Roosevelt

---

62. Patient 2366: G

DOC I hope you are ignoring your voices, now G

G Ignoring my voices?

DOC Ignoring T

G I could never ignore T. T is part of me

DOC I thought "T" was a problem.

G I have to listen to T otherwise I wouldn't be able to go
through the day.

DOC I hope "T" will advise you on how to interact with other
people

G I don't have a problem anymore: I just tell everyone what I
think when things need to be said

DOC I don't believe this is appropriate. People are what they
are; they can misunderstand you; they may have an
understanding problem, they can be ill. There is no need to be
rude to anyone.

G I'm never rude to anyone. But there is no reason why anyone has to suffer these people and not tell them what damages they do to themselves and to me and to other people by being so brain dead. I think the whole world is stupid. And these people need to face up to it. They even need to face up to their own death.

DOC I'm not sure what you are saying

G I'm saying that they need to face up to things and their own death. They need to be confronted with their stupidity and the damage they are causing. There is never an excuse for being stupid.

DOC G. You can't kill someone because the person is stupid. There wouldn't be many people left on the planet otherwise

G No. But they need to be made responsible for their actions. Someone has to tell them why they will die.

DOC Anyone will die at some point in their life!

G Yes. Anyone will: of all ages but that's a natural death. But when they have abused their own body or other people by their own stupidity, they need to be made aware why they are dying or why they will die. Frankly DOC you're like a bad computer game. But like in any computer game, there can only be one winner.

DOC *#Frowning his eyebrows and scratching his hair*

G Or not…Depending on how this develops and that's scary in itself: there can only be one winner at a computer game but the winner will always lose once at least afterwards so the winner can be a loser too in the end. There is something really wrong in this.

DOC #*DOC thought that all the confusion triggered by G disappeared with the last murder. He is presently more bewildered than ever. He is forcing himself a timid smile*

G #*The smile has been picked up by G and in turn G is returning his proverbial victory smile*

---

63. Patient 2166: ROOSEVELT

ROOSEVELT #*The interview isn't going very well. Mr Roosevelt is presently howling, unable to control his nerves*

DOC #*DOC is stunned and petrified, unable to move, he firmly believed that Mr Roosevelt had become a strong figure in recent months. DOC is completely shuttered: he cannot conceive that Mr Roosevelt can be that weak or might have this occasional moment of weakness*

DOC ROOSEVELT #*The howling lasts for 66 seconds, it's an absolutely horrendous sight.*

DOC's face turns red: an incredulous belief has been wiped out within a few moments. Could it be that he might have failed his patient in any way? A sense of doubt subsides. Which of his two T patients has presently failed him?

ROOSEVELT DOC #*Mr Roosevelt slowly regains control of himself but a few tears remain flowing over his face. He signals by waving his hand at DOC that it isn't the right time, gets up and leaves the room* *abandoning DOC by himself traumatised by what he has just witnessed.*

---

63. Patient 2366: G

G DOC!

DOC G, how are the voices today?

G My voice? That's very nice of you DOC to be concerned. T will be pleased.

DOC I'm sure he will. What I meant is are they steady, on an average level or higher?

G Steady and on an average level

DOC You haven't been crossed with anyone lately?

G Crossed?

DOC Upset or angry?

G No. Just the usual anger at some people over the phone. The usual.

DOC You mustn't get upset. You must show strength. I can understand your frustration but you must not let it go. Don't let it get over you! Some people are as they are, it's not their fault; it's what they have been taught, how they have been trained or it's how they were born.

G Oh I know that, DOC! Don't you worry. I only make sure they know where I stand and where they stand but I'm never angry. I never lose my temper in this way, that will show a weakness in me.

DOC I'm glad to hear it

---

64. Patient 2166: ROOSEVELT

DOC Mr Roosevelt!

ROOSEVELT DOC, I really need to apologise about my outburst yesterday. It's not like me. It shouldn't have happened. I wish it'd never happened and it's never gonna happen again. You mark my word!

DOC Mr Roosevelt. It was actually a very normal thing to do. You couldn't help it. We've been seeing each other for over two months. You've achieved so much; it was bound to happen and better here and now than later in the Senate.

ROOSEVELT I guess you're right DOC. It's still scary. I've never cried since I was a kid and never to that extent.

DOC It's good for your nerves, good for your eyes and you've released some unwanted toxins at the same time. Think about it in this way.

ROOSEVELT I will try.

DOC Please delete yesterday from your memory, if you can

ROOSEVELT T will never allow it but I'll try to ignore it.
Thanks, DOC!

DOC ....

---

64. Patient 2366: G

G Hey DOC! Time is running out. I will miss you

DOC No you won't. You despise me

G I hate you at times that is true but I will still miss our sessions.
I won't cry over you whether you're dead or alive, DOC!

#Offering DOC his "Victory" smile

DOC *#Returning G's smile with more rigour than he has ever
attempted before but still forced upon himself* G, tell me: have you
ever cried?

G Cried? What for?

DOC For anything...

G When I was a kid, maybe a few times maybe but what is the
point? Didn't you always say "to get on with it"? "Ignore things"
or because "we have to live with it"? So, what's the point in
crying?

DOC You've never shed a tear for your parents when they
died?

G My parents? They died years ago and they deserved it.

DOC What have they done to deserve it?

G They brought me to life. Think about that! What is really sad is that they died never knowing they deserved it. They both died of gas poisoning.

#Throwing his victorious "Victory" smile at DOC

DOC *#DOC is not returning any smiles. He is motionless and without any visible emotion; he simply doesn't know how to respond*

---

65. Patient 2166: ROOSEVELT

ROOSEVELT It has been a very strange couple of months in here, DOC

DOC I agree

It really helped to put my own house and my head in order and view things from a different perspective and I'm trying really hard to suppress those awful murders from my memory but they are not fading away that easily.

DOC It was very frightening. I myself am at a loss to explain what happened.

ROOSEVELT So scary. The victims have been killed with knives from the centre's kitchen

DOC From the centre's kitchen? *#Confused.* I didn't know about that

ROOSEVELT Yeah. Some of the victims had their ears chopped off

DOC Oh, No!

ROOSEVELT And one had an eye removed.

DOC I had no idea...

ROOSEVELT In all, they had 4 ears, 1 nose and 1 eye removed; 6 organs in total.

DOC *#DOC has just frozen stiff struggling to compose himself*

My God!

ROOSEVELT Yeah. I hope now that I've said all this aloud it will really fade out from my memory. It often works.

DOC *#DOC is unable to respond to this*

ROOSEVELT The killer must have been really desperate.

DOC *#DOC suddenly unfreezes* Desperate?

ROOSEVELT Possessed and completely oblivious of his actions.

DOC I suppose you're right

ROOSEVELT No one in their right mind would carry such a massacre!

DOC No!

ROOSEVELT The FBI believes that the removal of the organs occurred after the stabbing so they might have been dead already.

DOC God!

ROOSEVELT I hope they haven't suffered

DOC Yes a killer is often overpowered by a rage triggered by some events. I don't believe those people know what they are doing. They are possessed by a force beyond themselves.

ROOSEVELT That could be a fair assessment

---

65. Patient 2366: G

G I really miss Starbucks coffee here.

DOC Starbucks? It has been a while since you've last mentioned it.

G It's terrific. Even black and especially black. One short drip and you can run to the bathroom and overfill the place there. 2 coffees and it's multiple trips to the bathroom. I have to say that I have been a bit stuck here.

DOC I'm sorry to hear of your constipation problems. I had no idea about the effect that a Starbucks coffee can produce, it is worth noting for anyone on a diet.

G Diet?

DOC Anyone trying to lose weight

G They should just starve or live rough in the streets

DOC It's hard to starve

G It's easy when you're desperate

DOC Yes, I'm sorry. Starbucks coffee would seem to remain the best available option. In the meantime, I can organise some digestion tablets perhaps?

G No. It's alright DOC. I'll soon be away.

DOC Yes tomorrow!

G Yep *#For some reasons G doesn't throw his proverbial smile at DOC and ended the session without another word*

---

66. Patient 2166: ROOSEVELT

DOC Mr Roosevelt!

ROOSEVELT DOC!

DOC It has been 66 interviews!

ROOSEVELT Good God!

DOC I believe you'll be leaving the centre now

ROOSEVELT Yes, finally

DOC We'll be in touch. Please email me whenever you need it

ROOSEVELT I will DOC, Thank you

DOC It has been a privilege, Mr Roosevelt. Thank you.

ROOSEVELT Likewise

DOC I look forward to seeing you in the Senate!

ROOSEVELT Thanks, DOC!

---

66. Patient 2366: G

G DOC: I'm not sure what to say anymore: it is our last interview

DOC It is, G!

G 66 interviews!

DOC You have counted them?

G You bet I have

DOC Are you ready to face life on the outside, G?

G I am. More than ever. How about you DOC? Ready to face life and death?

DOC #*Confused* Yes, I suppose I am

G I'm glad to hear it, DOC!

#G ends his last meeting with DOC with his victorious smile

DOC *#DOC is struggling to return the smile*

G Well, Bye DOC! *#G is offering a hand shake*

DOC *#DOC is returning the hand shake*

Thank you, G., It has been an experience!

#DOC switches the lights off in the interview room for the last time.

ACT II: EMAILS

1.   **R_REPLIED**   Emails exchanged between Mr Roosevelt and DOC.
2.   **G_REPLIED**   Emails exchanged between G and DOC.

3. **R_Not REPLIED**   Emails sent by Mr Roosevelt to DOC but not replied.

4. **G_Not REPLIED**   Emails sent by G to DOC but not replied.

1. Email: R_REPLIED

DOC Dear Mr Roosevelt. Send me your questions and I'll try to help.

ROOSEVELT I don't have any questions.

2. Email: R_REPLIED

DOC You don't?

ROOSEVELT I think it's pretty clear what's happening here.

3. Email: R_REPLIED

DOC What is happening?

ROOSEVELT I've been possessed.

DOC It is one way of looking at it.

ROOSEVELT A sure way. That's exactly what is happening here DOC!

5. Email: R_REPLIED

DOC There are many causes that lead to your condition.

ROOSEVELT Causes?

6. Email: R_REPLIED

DOC Symptoms…

ROOSEVELT Yeah, sure. Someone or something moved inside my brain. You can call it "symptoms".

DOC T is not altogether a new condition but we've only recently recognized it as a condition.

ROOSEVELT Before people were locked up and lobotomized inside an asylum!

8. Email: R_REPLIED

DOC I wouldn't put it that way!

ROOSEVELT Where else? Area 51? Or is it 61?

9. Email: R_REPLIED

DOC If you're hearing voices then people can have a great cause for concern.

ROOSEVELT I don't hear voices. The voices are inside my brain. They hear me and I can hear this and they are listening to me hearing them.

10. Email: R_REPLIED

DOC These voices... What are they saying?

ROOSEVELT I don't understand space-alien languages!

11. Email: R_REPLIED

DOC Space aliens?

ROOSEVELT It's not in English and it's probably not a language as in "speaking" language.

12. Email: R_REPLIED

DOC Fair enough. So, if it is not a language, is it just a sound?

ROOSEVELT You know damn well it is a sound.

13. Email: R_REPLIED

DOC Everything you hear is a sound.

ROOSEVELT A sound is not necessarily spoken and not by a human.

14. Email: R_REPLIED

ROOSEVELT The sound is still talking and it's not human.

DOC How can you tell it's talking and it's not human?

15. Email: R_REPLIED

ROOSEVELT Because this sound has a way to guide me, disturb me and move me from beyond any terrestrial and human power.

DOC So you're possessed?

16. Email: R_REPLIED

ROOSEVELT Yes!

DOC By alien forces?

17. Email: R_REPLIED

ROOSEVELT Yes!

DOC We're finally getting somewhere.

18. Email: R_REPLIED

ROOSEVELT Finally!

DOC So you no longer have T?

19. Email: R_REPLIED

ROOSEVELT That's what T is!

DOC What is T?

20. Email: R_REPLIED

ROOSEVELT   Extra-terrestrial. A thing beyond human. Not organic.

DOC If you're hearing voices you might be declared insane.

21. Email: R_REPLIED

ROOSEVELT I know and I'm not.

DOC I do believe you have T.

ROOSEVELT I know

DOC I'm glad we've agreed.

23. Email: R_REPLIED

ROOSEVELT Glad? I haven't slept in a week and you're glad?

DOC I can help with that.

24. Email: R_REPLIED

ROOSEVELT No thanks. I don't want to become a complete zombie.

DOC What do you want?

25. Email: R_REPLIED

ROOSEVELT I want you to release me from them DOC!

DOC Them?

26. Email: R_REPLIED

ROOSEVELT The alien forces: T!

DOC It's a condition and not an illness. Most people are born
with it.

27. Email: R_REPLIED

ROOSEVELT I don't know if I was born with it.

DOC It must have been silent and a series of events could have
triggered and provoked this.

28. Email: R_REPLIED

ROOSEVELT I could believe that.

DOC Ignore it, get on with it.

29. Email: R_REPLIED

ROOSEVELT Ignore it? A highway in full action 24/7?

DOC Ignore it!

30. Email: R_REPLIED

ROOSEVELT I do! I try each second of the day but it's still there.

DOC Try harder!

31. Email: R_REPLIED

ROOSEVELT Harder?

DOC Harder!

32. Email: R_REPLIED

ROOSEVELT Harder than this?

DOC Harder than this!

33. Email: R_REPLIED

ROOSEVELT And when I have a headache? It's like having a hangover!

DOC Ignore it! Take an aspirin and get on with it!

34. Email: R_REPLIED

ROOSEVELT I do and it's still there.

DOC Don't drink!

---

35. Email: R_REPLIED

ROOSEVELT I don't drink!

DOC How do you know about hangovers?

---

36. Email: R_REPLIED

ROOSEVELT I was young once!

DOC Don't drink and don't smoke!

---

37. Email: R_REPLIED

ROOSEVELT I don't! How can I possibly smoke with T? It would only kill me instantly.

DOC T sufferers can't drink and can't smoke.

38. Email: R_REPLIED

ROOSEVELT Lucky for me that I do neither.

DOC Ignore T! Get on with your life!

39. Email: R_REPLIED

ROOSEVELT Trust me I do but it's still there!

DOC It will always be there! Ignore it!

40. Email: R_REPLIED

ROOSEVELT This is not really getting us anywhere! It's like I'm interacting with a robot. We've been through it all before!

DOC

41. Email: R_REPLIED

DOC It does get us somewhere. You confirmed it!

ROOSEVELT How did I confirm anything?

42. Email: R_REPLIED

DOC By ignoring it.

ROOSEVELT I have to. If I don't, I die.

43. Email: R_REPLIED

DOC It's the only way to survive.

ROOSEVELT I know.

44. Email: R_REPLIED

DOC You can't fight T! Just ignore it!

ROOSEVELT It's easier when you have some money I guess.

45. Email: R_REPLIED

DOC It's irrelevant. It's your own will.

ROOSEVELT Irrelevant? If you can't work you can't live!

46. Email: R_REPLIED

DOC It's your own willingness to survive. Not a question of money.

ROOSEVELT I don't believe this. Lucky for me I have some money.

47. Email: R_REPLIED

DOC Just ignore T.

ROOSEVELT I do, DOC! TRUST ME I'M TRYING TO! But T will never go away!

48. Email: R_REPLIED

DOC T will never go away. NEVER. Just ignore it!

ROOSEVELT I do!

49. Email: R_REPLIED

DOC Good!

ROOSEVELT Good?

50. Email: R_REPLIED

DOC Yes, it's good!

ROOSEVELT It wasn't so good when you inflicted your sound therapy on me DOC! It made matters worse: it amplified it like there is no tomorrow!

51. Email: R_REPLIED

DOC This was your own choice!

ROOSEVELT My choice?

DOC Sound therapy was a way to alleviate your condition. It generally helps. Well, it didn't in your case. You seem to be an exceptional case.

ROOSEVELT Am I?

DOC Yes!

ROOSEVELT Maybe, just maybe you could do with a little twist in your sobriety DOC?

DOC ....

55. Email: R_REPLIED

ROOSEVELT Some humility wouldn't go amiss!

DOC ....

56. Email: R_REPLIED

ROOSEVELT If you could lower yourself a bit from your own pedestal, maybe?

DOC ....

57. Email: R_REPLIED

ROOSEVELT Why be so arrogant?

DOC ....

58. Email: R_REPLIED

ROOSEVELT   You're expensive enough!

DOC ...

59. Email: R_REPLIED

ROOSEVELT   That's precisely my sentiment!

DOC .... ?

60. Email: R_REPLIED

ROOSEVELT   Oh, a question mark now?

DOC ....

61. Email: R_REPLIED

ROOSEVELT You might have planted T whilst I was in your care at the centre DOC

DOC I thought you had it before?

62. Email: R_REPLIED

ROOSEVELT   It may have been something else but during my stay at the centre I've moved to a point of no return.

DOC ....

63. Email: R_REPLIED

ROOSEVELT I believe you are T!

DOC ....

64. Email: R_REPLIED

ROOSEVELT How do you do it DOC from a distance?

DOC ....

65. Email: R_REPLIED

ROOSEVELT   Are you extra-terrestrial, DOC?

DOC ....

66. Email: R_REPLIED

ROOSEVELT Where are you DOC?

DOC ....

2. G_REPLIED

1. Email: G_REPLIED

G   Hi DOC! Got any pills? I don't smoke. I can't smoke as you know so it seems fair enough. Jesus if I was smoking the smoke will torture T then I'll get even more tortured in return.

DOC I can't prescribe any medication for your condition.

2. Email: G_REPLIED

G What have you got for me DOC?

DOC I'm here for you

3. Email: G_REPLIED

G Where?

DOC Here!

4. Email: G_REPLIED

G How can you be fucking here when you're not there?

    DOC Please don't swear at me!

5. Email: G_REPLIED

G What the fuck?

DOC I'm here to help you but I can't and I won't help you if you start yelling abuses at me.

6. Email: G_REPLIED

G Touchy man!

DOC ....

---

7. Email: G_REPLIED

G What does "...." mean?

DOC Do you have any questions for me?

---

8. Email: G_REPLIED

G Do you have a girlfriend?

DOC I'm not here to answer private questions!

---

9. Email: G_REPLIED

G Are you really ready for any questions DOC?

DOC I'm all yours Gordon

10. Email: G_REPLIED

G What is T?

DOC You know what it is

11. Email: G_REPLIED

G What is T?

DOC T is not a who

12. Email: G_REPLIED

G Not who?

DOC You can't define it

DOC T is a phenomenon that occurs inside your brain and you can only be aware of it because it creates some sounds through your ears.

G Well done DOC! As if I didn't know. What I wanna know is: can you kill it?

14. Email: G_REPLIED

DOC You can't kill it.

G Can't?

15. Email: G_REPLIED

DOC Can't!

G T is killing me.

16. Email: G_REPLIED

DOC Yes and very slowly if you let it.

G I have to let it go. I have no other choice.

17. Email: G_REPLIED

DOC In life we always have a choice.

G Like what?

18. Email: G_REPLIED

DOC Ignore it.

G Fuck that... When it controls me and I fall on the floor and roll around screaming and shaking I have to ignore it?

---

19. Email: G_REPLIED

DOC Ignore it!

G I even remember every time T shows up. That's a lot of repeat DOC!

---

20. Email: G_REPLIED

DOC Ignore it!

G That's like all the fucking TV repeats!

---

21. Email: G_REPLIED

DOC Ignore it!

G And how am I supposed to do this DOC?

22. Email: G_REPLIED

DOC Don't think about it!

G T thinks for me. It controls my brain and my thoughts.

23. Email: G_REPLIED

DOC Ignore it!

G It gets worse when I watch TV

24. Email: G_REPLIED

DOC Don't watch TV

G That's the only thing I can do.

25. Email: G_REPLIED

DOC Read.

G Read?

26. Email: G_REPLIED

G   I can't read!

DOC Learn to read!

27. Email: G_REPLIED

G Learn? And who will be fucking paying for me to learn?

DOC Welfare has a program for it. It's free.

G Fucking read! Who wants to read shit?

DOC There are a lot of good books around.

29. Email: G_REPLIED

G Good! Then read them to me. And another thing: I can't work.

DOC Learn to work.

30. Email: G_REPLIED

G Learn to work? I know how to work, man! I can't work with T in my brain fucking me up all the time.

DOC I'm sorry, G. I meant

31. Email: G_REPLIED

DOC Ignore it

G I can't do anything. I can type and read but the only thing I read is so crap so I can't be bothered and I don't get it.

32. Email: G_REPLIED

DOC Walk!

G Walk? Walking on the moon?

33. Email: G_REPLIED

DOC Not on the moon. On Earth.

G I got that. It was a joke. You don't do jokes, do you DOC?

34. Email: G_REPLIED

DOC ....

G "...." Again?

35. Email: G_REPLIED

DOC ....

G How much are you getting paid DOC?

36. Email: G_REPLIED

DOC I'm not in a position to disclose.

G Can you lend me some cash?

37. Email: G_REPLIED

DOC ....

G Money will help me to kill T!

38. Email: G_REPLIED

DOC No, it wouldn't

G Do you hate me DOC?

39. Email: G_REPLIED

DOC ....

G T is killing me

40. Email: G_REPLIED

DOC Don't let it!

G I will

41. Email: G_REPLIED

DOC Don't

G I'm already in full process

42. Email: G_REPLIED

DOC Ignore it!

G Fuck it and fuck you!

43. Email: G_REPLIED

DOC ....

G You can ignore this. I can't!

DOC You can!

G I CAN'T!

DOC Yes you can!

G "Yes you can"? What's that? A coffee commercial?

DOC ....

G ...

47. Email: G_REPLIED

G .... ?

DOC I'm trying to level you.

48. Email: G_REPLIED

G What great therapy. I couldn't have done any better DOC!

DOC ....

49. Email: G_REPLIED

G ....

DOC ....

50. Email: G_REPLIED

G Fuck T! I can't even drink! If get drunk I start screaming

DOC Don't drink.

51. Email: G_REPLIED

G Don't drink, don't fuck! What else?

DOC ....

52. Email: G_REPLIED

G Do you fuck DOC? Like fucking a girl?

DOC ....

53. Email: G_REPLIED

G I thought you wouldn't. DOC! Fucking boys?

DOC ....

54. Email: G_REPLIED

G   I thought you might!

DOC ....

55. Email: G_REPLIED

G "Might"! I'm not sure if it is a word. I've picked it up from you when you said it during our interviews at the centre.

DOC ....

56. Email: G_REPLIED

G DOC?

DOC ....

57. Email: G_REPLIED

G I'm sure you're T and you're the one fucking with my brain. I should fucking kill ya!

DOC ....

58. Email: G_REPLIED

G DOC?

DOC ....

G   I'm finding it hard to believe that it is your DOC. You are not there. You were never there!

DOC

G It's easy not to answer. Even back at the centre you never really tried and you never knew what really went on around you. You can't be that fucking blind!

DOC ....

G Silence is no excuse ; it's only the beginning of the problem. For sure, silence will be responsible for your actions but you will need to face up to why you yourself will be silenced in the end.

DOC ...

62. Email: G_REPLIED

G DOC: following my last email, you need to confront what you did otherwise you'll never know why you'll be silenced.

DOC ...

63. Email: G_REPLIED

G You've offered me this exchange, not the other way around and yet you seem to have walked away from this offer. An offer is an offer and I have taken your offer!

64. Email: G_REPLIED

G I'm really losing my patience with you, DOC!

65. Email: G_REPLIED

G You can't escape me, DOC!

66. Email: G_REPLIED

G Any last words?

3. G_Not REPLIED

1. Email: G_Not_REPLIED

G When I woke up this morning my whole body trembled, I felt pins and needles and I felt like a sudden rush of blood forcing its way through my brain.

It has happened before. Many times. Then my vision was all blurry and my eyes felt as heavy as bricks are. The sound of one hundred birds came tweeting inside my ears, from the inside that is. I sat on the edge of the bed.

I stayed still in apparent silence. I have disturbed a whole orchestra of fucking birds and generally when there is an orchestra playing the public shuts the fuck up. I coughed and sneezed maybe but I sat in silence hoping for the sound of silence to arise.

I just wish people would leave me alone. Just wish T would finally leave me alone instead of conducting some fucking orchestra or was it just an extra-terrestrial conference on the best way to fuck someone up from within the brain.

We're already force fed with crap all day long. We're already told what to do, what to be and what to think.

If the brain is all controlled then where else can anyone go? Away from the Eagle's view. Where else?

I'm still investigating.

2. Email: G_Not_REPLIED

G I've passed another string of fucking police's sirens today.

Like the ambulance and the fire brigade's sirens: they are piercing through my brain. It's not the sound itself, it's loud enough but it's beyond deafening. It's rocket fuel passing through my brain.

It's so trenchant, it vibrates inside the head then I hear the sound of breaking glass. For each sound of a siren fired, it triggers the sound of 10 breaking glasses. About that and it lingers on for an hour or two.

Should I sue them all? Fucking cops!

3. Email: G_Not_REPLIED

G Fucking you as well. You have failed to reply to many of my emails. What are you trying to do to me?

My ears are numb now and have been for the whole day.

I'm like deaf, half deaf. I have tried to clean my ears but couldn't find a Q-tip so I've used a pen. The wax inside is revolting if you think about it. It's worse than plain shit. At least with shit you don't feel like checking it too closely because of the stench.

Anyway after cleaning my ears I still felt completely numbed at ear level. I can't really hear anything from the outside but only from the inside. From inside my brain: it started with water flowing then it progressively moved to a jet flying too low and is about to crash over a city killing at least 100 people and injuring 200.

---

4. Email: G_Not_REPLIED

G OK, DOC! What are you up to? What are you really up to? You can't just abandon your patients like this! If I had your phone number, I could call you but I don't. I know you're still getting my emails since they haven't been returned. You may be dead; I have no way of finding out since you no longer work at the Center.

Come on, DOC! You can do better than this!

---

5. Email: G_Not_REPLIED

G Rain today. Raining hard both inside my brain and outside. At least I can't hear the fucking rain outside, only inside my brain. I wouldn't be able to handle both at the same time.

There was a guy who said "flipping rain" today in the streets. "Flipping rain" I've never heard of this before.

"Flipping rain" that's a good one.

6. Email: G_Not_REPLIED

G I'm still here. The rain inside my brain is turning into some kind of voice. Fucking voices and I can't understand it. It's not very loud but it's still there.

7. Email: G_Not_REPLIED

G Still raining: God I can hear some of the rain outside in the streets now and the rain inside my head and the voices inside are getting louder. Fucking voices. There are voices all right but I can't hear what they are saying.

8. Email: G_Not_REPLIED

G The voices inside me are more than just a noise. "They" are "voices".

G It has been 9 days without hearing from you and my brain
is still fucked up. When my brain will be completely fucked
up I'll send you a bill for the surgery.

Are you not supposed to be my DOC?

G OK, DOC! Where are you? Fucking sun tanning yourself
with drugs and bitches? Boys in your case.

DOC! I'm only asking you for a reply!

G You're a fucking idiot DOC. That's all I can say! You kept
on asking me if I was scared. Scared of what?

Scared of you? Why should I be scared? I'm not scared. I'm not hurt as such, I'm not dead yet or in fear of my life or in fear of death. I'm just having my brain overtaken by alien forces and no one can do anything about it and no one believe me or give a fuck.

---

12. Email: G_Not_REPLIED

G I rectify from yesterday's email: there are not alien forces but ghosts! Ghosts in the machine. Aliens can be identifiable but ghosts can't. They come and they go as they please and do what they fucking want. I just want them to fuck off from my brain. That's why I came to you. DOC!

---

13. Email: G_Not_REPLIED

G   Ghosts. That's what they are DOC and they are having an annual get-together inside my brain. The only fucking problem is that the get-together is fucking around the clock. Last night they partied all night. It was like inside a highway and the noises were like peak time. All fucking up in a big orgy with drugs and very loud music.

My brain is such a filthy place. The music stinks: it's just loud noises but it's also music blasting all night.

G How can I possibly get a job when all this screwing is going on inside my brain? I still have some cash from a break I did years ago. Yeah. Don't fucking patronize me DOC: welfare and work are over for people fucked up like me. I can't work and if I can't work how can I fucking pay my way? Answer me that one, DOC!

I need some fucking cash! You're not helping and you get paid for my treatment by a charity office. They pay our bills, they pay your rent, for now but at least you have a job.

Don't panic, I'm not addicted to breaking into any folks' houses. I will only do it again when the money is running out.

I gotta do it DOC no one else will do it for me: gotta have to pay my way, DOC!

15. Email: G_Not_REPLIED

G Rich idiots don't care if they have less money, they just make more. SO, it's fucking all right!

16. Email: G_Not_REPLIED

G I've been a rough sleeper before and I've been in various jails before. 5 times since I was 12. I prefer sleeping in jails than in the streets. Rich people when they are drunk or stoned, they come and howl abuses at you when you are lying on the floor and they kick you to death. It happened to me once. I was so wounded I had to crawl on the floor and the bruises lasted for a few months after that. In jail most people got some form of T. It's violent too but never mingle with anyone and just please anyone; that's the only way to survive there and it's free. Free inside the jail, free from paying any rent or any lousy food. Food is crap wherever you go, at least in jail it's free.

17. Email: G_Not_REPLIED

G I'm not even hungry anymore. I'm as skinny as a nail. A fucking nail. How come? I can't sleep, I do eat crap sometimes and yet I'm still standing. How come, DOC? Yeah, you! You're the DOC! Too fucked up are you?

18. Email: G_Not_REPLIED

G Playing hard to get, are you, DOC? Come on DOC! Reply to my fucking emails pussy and don't expect a fucking blow job!

19. Email: G_Not_REPLIED

G I can hear some words now from the voices. Words that I don't understand but there are words.

20. Email: G_Not_REPLIED

G Words don't count but the ghosts are trying to tell me something. I know they are: they fucking are!

21. Email: G_Not_REPLIED

G I can't get on with it and never will. Give me six years down in time. Six years at best and I'll be dead.

It's a fight between two forces and there can be only one winner. Fuck life! There can always be only one winner.

I'm too poor and already too fucked up to survive it. Fucked up man!

---

22. Email: G_Not_REPLIED

G I can fucking kill you for ignoring my emails. I can sue you DOC and get enough cash to survive until T kills me completely. Sue you, DOC! Fuck you!

---

23. Email: G_Not_REPLIED

G You're a fucking shithead like all the other fuckers. You
pretend things, pretend that you can do many things but the
reality is you can't. You just steal money from people. That's
theft. That's fucking criminal. I do the same but at least I'm
truthful about this. Some people are paying for you to help me
and you can't do fuck all.

24. Email: G_Not_REPLIED

G I will kill you. This is a fact. Fuck you! Fuck them all! T is a
government thing: must be. Who wants to control people?

Fuck them, fuck you. Fuck them all!

25. Email: G_Not_REPLIED

G I haven't decided how to kill you yet, DOC. Instant death or
slow death. Slow death will take weeks.

26. Email: G_Not_REPLIED

G Tell me, DOC! Fucking tell me before I put you to death.
Reply to me! Fucking reply to me!!!!!!!!!

27. Email: G_Not_REPLIED

G You're dead, I'm nearly dead. So, what the fuck?

28. Email: G_Not_REPLIED

G I can't even fuck a girl anymore. T is there: watching me and
telling me what to do. I know "it" does. I can't understand it
but I just know it. Who wants to fuck with a whole audience
inside the brain?

29. Email: G_Not_REPLIED

G Fuck you DOC! I even have you in my fucking brain: you're
here all the time in my fucking brain. Fucking memory.

I can see you and all our sessions. The whole fucking movie:

every second of it. Everything like if it was yesterday.

Why is that, DOC? Why DOC? Why did you do this to me?
Did you fucking open my brain while I was asleep at the
center?

30. Email: G_Not_REPLIED

G What have you done to me, DOC? You will tell me before I
kill you.

31. Email: G_Not_REPLIED

G

I will kill you, DOC!

I will kill you, DOC!

I will kill you, DOC!

I will kill you, DOC!

I will kill you, DOC!

I will kill you, DOC!

32. Email: G_Not_REPLIED

G

I will kill you, DOC!

I will kill you, DOC!

I will kill you, DOC!

I will kill you, DOC!

I will kill you, DOC!

I will kill you, DOC!

33. Email: G_Not_REPLIED

G

I will kill you, DOC!

I will kill you, DOC!

I will kill you, DOC!

I will kill you, DOC!

I will kill you, DOC!

I will kill you, DOC!

34. Email: G_Not_REPLIED

G

I will kill you, DOC!

I will kill you, DOC!

I will kill you, DOC!

I will kill you, DOC!

I will kill you, DOC!

I will kill you, DOC!

35. Email: G_Not_REPLIED

G

I will kill you, DOC!

I will kill you, DOC!

I will kill you, DOC!

I will kill you, DOC!

I will kill you, DOC!

I will kill you, DOC!

G

I will kill you, DOC!

I will kill you, DOC!

I will kill you, DOC!

I will kill you, DOC!

I will kill you, DOC!

I will kill you, DOC!

37. Email: G_Not_REPLIED

G I will die soon anyway, so what the fuck? T will kill me.

38. Email: G_Not_REPLIED

G

T will kill me.

T will kill me.

T will kill me.

T will kill me.

T will kill me.

T will kill me.

---

39. Email: G_Not_REPLIED

G

T will kill me.

T will kill me.

T will kill me.

T will kill me.

T will kill me.

T will kill me.

G

T will kill me.

T will kill me.

T will kill me.

T will kill me.

T will kill me.

T will kill me.

G

T will kill me.

T will kill me.

T will kill me.

T will kill me.

T will kill me.

T will kill me.

G

T will kill me.

T will kill me.

T will kill me.

T will kill me.

T will kill me.

T will kill me.

G

T will kill me.

T will kill me.

T will kill me.

T will kill me.

T will kill me.

T will kill me.

G

I'm gonna kill you.

I'm gonna kill you.

I'm gonna kill you.

I'm gonna kill you.

I'm gonna kill you.

I'm gonna kill you.

G

I'm gonna kill you.

I'm gonna kill you.

I'm gonna kill you.

I'm gonna kill you.

I'm gonna kill you.

I'm gonna kill you.

G

I'm gonna kill you.

I'm gonna kill you.

I'm gonna kill you.

I'm gonna kill you.

I'm gonna kill you.

I'm gonna kill you.

G

I'm gonna kill you.

I'm gonna kill you.

I'm gonna kill you.

I'm gonna kill you.

I'm gonna kill you.

I'm gonna kill you.

G

I'm gonna kill you.

I'm gonna kill you.

I'm gonna kill you.

I'm gonna kill you.

I'm gonna kill you.

I'm gonna kill you.

G

I'm gonna kill you.

I'm gonna kill you.

I'm gonna kill you.

I'm gonna kill you.

I'm gonna kill you.

I'm gonna kill you.

G

And then I will be DEAD.

And then I will be DEAD.

And then I will be DEAD.

And then I will be DEAD.

And then I will be DEAD.

And then I will be DEAD.

G

And then I will be DEAD.

And then I will be DEAD.

And then I will be DEAD.

And then I will be DEAD.

And then I will be DEAD.

And then I will be DEAD.

G

And then I will be DEAD.

And then I will be DEAD.

And then I will be DEAD.

And then I will be DEAD.

And then I will be DEAD.

And then I will be DEAD.

G

And then I will be DEAD.

And then I will be DEAD.

And then I will be DEAD.

And then I will be DEAD.

And then I will be DEAD.

And then I will be DEAD.

G

And then I will be DEAD.

And then I will be DEAD.

And then I will be DEAD.

And then I will be DEAD.

And then I will be DEAD.

And then I will be DEAD.

G

And then I will be DEAD.

And then I will be DEAD.

And then I will be DEAD.

And then I will be DEAD.

And then I will be DEAD.

And then I will be DEAD.

G DEAD. Maybe not then and there but later on. I'm not making any predictions but say in about six years.

It's how long I know I will survive and 6 is my number.

You add 6 years then you end up with another 6 for T and you face the beast and then you kill the beast.

The beast can only be killed. T will be killed and I will be killed with it.

57. Email: G_Not_REPLIED

G

I will kill T.

I will kill T.

I will kill T.

I will kill T.

I will kill T.

I will kill T.

58. Email: G_Not_REPLIED

G

I will kill T.

I will kill T.

I will kill T.

I will kill T.

I will kill T.

I will kill T.

59. Email: G_Not_REPLIED

G

I will kill T.

I will kill T.

I will kill T.

I will kill T.

I will kill T.

I will kill T.

60. Email: G_Not_REPLIED

G

I will kill T.

I will kill T.

I will kill T.

I will kill T.

I will kill T.

I will kill T.

61. Email: G_Not_REPLIED

G

I will kill T.

I will kill T.

I will kill T.

I will kill T.

I will kill T.

I will kill T.

---

62. Email: G_Not_REPLIED

G

I will kill T.

I will kill T.

I will kill T.

I will kill T.

I will kill T.

I will kill T.

63. Email: G_Not_REPLIED

G Are you still there, DOC?

64. Email: G_Not_REPLIED

G DOC, are you dead now? DOC?

65. Email: G_Not_REPLIED

G We all have to die at some point in time. DOC.

G I'll see you in hell, DOC

<u>Mail failure, return to sender</u>

Delivery to the following recipient failed permanently:

----- Original message -----

X--DKIM-Signature: v=1; a=rsa-sh; c=relaxed/relaxed;

d=dickhead.com; s=20120113;

h=mime-version:sender:x-originating-ip:date:x-dick-sender-auth

:message-id:subject:from:to:content-type:x-gm-message-state;

bh=DFxcm5SqHZMDvG+geuEg71554tTl/04qGk1VFg=;

b=SkTaRFIwl6xJaI6DkGr7dMYMu2koeRn1lxmOWMUZEzJA
T6nid4QcOWwM0HJKaSzhDZ

InJ2MAix8/7sg65qkVLeIjCAkBuen0Rpm10FkZK/+Dng9V4A/7
h7ue3Kib2j

9+RrlPpknL1E+Bsz37CG3HDLnn1c45dy+mulxh1m0iwCDf2Z1
zTV5CBtHxLH

4NGmAV2ADirVnND6A0GkheL68XLfU3Te2xVabFEeIN0INd
X0Nyp09pkOoyRH

jS4Iz6lq37r36xpysgPrpgWBZkzpuL3WT1tFpz3mKdpJ9F

URxA==

MIME-Version: 1.0

Received: by 10.204.148.72 with SMTP id
o8mr2926180bkv.127.1339777066763; Fri,

15 Jun 2012 09:17:46 -0700 (PDT)

Sender: G

Received: by 10.205.26.6 with HTTP; Fri, 15 Jun 2012 09:17:44 -
0700 (PDT)

X-Originating-IP: [657]

Date: Fri, 15 Jun 2012 17:17:44 +0100

X--Sender-Auth: gH6pp7krxM

Message-ID: <CuwqJCka+gtjeXSv_jg@dick.com>

Subject: Follow up Treatment

From: G <g@g>

To: DOC@DOC

Content-Type: multipart/mixed;
boundary=0015175cab32248a6d04c285287c

X-Gm-Message-State:
ALoCoQnVt1nBTE8BCDdkh2hjr44uqOD9xJSl

3. R_Not REPLIED

1. Email: R_Not_REPLIED

ROOSEVELT   I find being alone extremely oppressing. Being alone is also a necessary evil. I can't stand people. I hate people and when I see someone, I just ignore the person. I ignore my family most of the time and I haven't got any friends. It's much easier that way.

When lightning strikes me, the noise is so unbearable I wouldn't be able to hide my pain and I can quickly become unbearable to be with.

Alone is hell; it's close to dying but it's still safer than being in close vicinity of a human being.

I can't even stand dogs or cats either.

---

2. Email: R_Not_REPLIED

ROOSEVELT I can't talk to anyone about my condition. No one would understand. It's despairing. Maybe the brain is a power station now, maybe it's muting into a new being. If that is the case, it needs to hurry up. I can't sleep or I can. That's the point; I sleep around midnight and by this stage I'm very tired but I wake up every two hours and I hear birds, birds inside my brain.

3. Email: R_Not_REPLIED

ROOSEVELT I can still hear the birds and it's deafening. What I haven't heard is something from you. I have sent you a few emails but you have not responded as yet. Are you away?

4. Email: R_Not_REPLIED

ROOSEVELT I wouldn't say that I worry about the noise, I'm more concerned about becoming deaf and I can still do my everyday things. It's just so deafening sometimes. I remember what you said to me: "I have to keep on going, I have to ignore it. " If I want to move on but if I can't sleep, how on earth am I going to carry on during the day!

5. Email: R_Not_REPLIED

ROOSEVELT I'm all yours. Mr., I forgot your name. I used to call you DOC and I've never actually called you from your real name. What is your name? Your email is not that revealing: 666times2@ . That's not a name!

Are you still seeing other patients?

---

6. Email: R_Not_REPLIED

ROOSEVELT Why can't you reply to my emails? I'm still paying for the bill. I've received one recently from the Medical Centre. It's strange that they never mention your name. But you do exist, don't you? I remember you very well. That's another point: that noise, this machine inside my brain is triggering strange things: I start remembering things. Everything since I was born. Meaningless crap like the ATM machine I've been to 6 years ago, 6 months ago or even last year. The slight pain I felt in a muscle 6 years ago. I remember the taste of things as well. It's vivid. There is no yesterday or the day before inside my brain. It's instant; all mixed up together.

What's really happening here?

7. Email: R_Not_REPLIED

ROOSEVELT Water is flowing inside. Niagara Falls more like it. I can almost hear someone screaming or crying but it's not very clear. It could be anything.

8. Email: R_Not_REPLIED

ROOSEVELT Jesus. I'm fucked. The noise is constant now and I can hear voices now. That's the first sign of madness hearing voices. I can hear entire conversations but it's too fast. It could be conversations I took part in at some point in time or a conversation from a film. There are voices but I can't understand them. I can't even understand any words but I just know there are conversations and very lengthy ones like that.

9. Email: R_Not_REPLIED

ROOSEVELT I don't have your number Mystery DOC but I know you are receiving my emails. They are not sent back in return.

It's like talking to a brick wall! Are you taking notes, DOC?

I've called the Medical Centre and you are still technically employed there but are away for a few months.

So where are you exactly?

I have mentioned that you haven't replied to my emails and said that the centre still billed me for treatment but they said the bill was for the previous months.

It's now an airport inside my brain. Planes flying, planes crashing, passengers waiting, running, screaming, eating, going to the bathroom and agonising. And where are you in the middle of all this?

Can you answer this DOC? Can you really?

10. Email: R_Not_REPLIED

ROOSEVELT I now have the United Nations inside my brain. An emergency session and every single delegate is arguing with one another and talking at the same time and there is no stopping them.

I thought it was your job to stop them, DOC! My brain is being invaded and you can't even help me.

I can't talk to anyone about this. No one would believe me. But the people are there; THEY are definitely there.

---

11. Email: R_Not_REPLIED

ROOSEVELT Am I talking to myself here? Writing to myself: I wouldn't even be able to hear myself anyway. Too busy and too loud inside my brain. It's so deafening inside and I'm already half deaf!

---

12. Email: R_Not_REPLIED

ROOSEVELT It's a problem when things are old. One answer generally triggers another question. I was never comfortable answering your questions DOC, as I knew you would be asking even more questions. One answer can be complicated enough and will take too long to explain. Questions are pointless. I believe like any psychiatrist; you are too sceptical and would never believe the patient. You doubt. Why should I be doubted? I'm the one with the problem, not you. Mind you: having doubts and doubting your patients is one problem so you have problems of your own.

At this rate a treatment can last forever and matters are sent to a point of no return when a doctor prescribes some chemicals. It's rather an odd concept: treating an imbalance of the brain with chemicals or even worse: surgery.

Who can really tell how the brain will react? T is not psychological. Something or someone has overtaken your brain remotely and unless you know who or what did this it's virtually impossible to treat. It's a condition.

Meanwhile, it's the sound of a highway in full action but just after the evening rush hour. Bearable I suppose but loud enough nonetheless.

---

13. Email: R_Not_REPLIED

ROOSEVELT It's like a draft of wind now. It's rather blasting on and off. Not like a fan but definitively the wind.

---

14. Email: R_Not_REPLIED

ROOSEVELT Following my last email, it's no longer the wind. It's a Typhoon now. Yes, definitely a Typhoon. The sound is coming out from my right ear. I mean I always had some trouble hearing from my left ear. Sometimes it happens abruptly then it restarts after a while. Then it's back on, on and off, off and on every 30 seconds.

15. Email: R_Not_REPLIED

ROOSEVELT I won't let this wind overtake my brain; whatever or whoever this force is trying to overpower my brain. My whole inner machine is being controlled but I will fight "them" every step of the way. If you let that thing win, you're totally controlled and dead.

16. Email: R_Not_REPLIED

ROOSEVELT Wind, water and air: all the elements are passing through my brain and my left ear, at least not as a physical and organic force I hope, but in noises and in spirits. Before I go to bed it's often an explosion followed by the sound of an earthquake hovering over and over again swiftly followed by the sound of a large river flowing continuously and mercilessly to a point of no return.

17. Email: R_Not_REPLIED

ROOSEVELT Sometimes I can hear words being shouted
away. Deep down I can hear entire conversations. Who are
these people? I can't figure it out. I can't understand what they
are saying and I can't hear them. They are just there: like
ghosts in the machine.

18. Email: R_Not_REPLIED

ROOSEVELT I'm officially possessed by T and there is
nothing anyone can do about it. There are no laws against
illegal immigrants and ghosts squatting your brain.

I can only suffer it or them and ignore it. It is better to just call
it "T"; it summarises the whole problem.

I can't and won't let T win. It's either T or me: if T wins I die
and if T dies, I win. Simple.

19. Email: R_Not_REPLIED

ROOSEVELT And it rains again on the outside, that is in the real world, on this planet we're all living. When it rains, because of T I get a splitting headache turning into a day-migraine when the sun makes an appearance.

---

20. Email: R_Not_REPLIED

ROOSEVELT When I was little I always wanted to die: I had to suffer in silence. No one would understand, it was only a figment of my imagination. I didn't think I was born to enjoy torture and born with an inherent desire to love being tortured.

---

21. Email: R_Not_REPLIED

ROOSEVELT I know you believe that patients are ill and sick and deeply troubled and be as it may, how do you explain why we've never chosen to have T and we were probably born this way?

---

22. Email: R_Not_REPLIED

ROOSEVELT I was born this way. No doubt about it. I had it
as far back as I can remember and since I'm aware of T, I
remember everything since I was born. Remembering how it
was, remembering how it all started...

---

23. Email: R_Not_REPLIED

ROOSEVELT I became aware of my condition in the last six
years. It was a gradual thing. I thought I was getting deaf from
my left ear then from both ears and it wasn't deafness after all,
it was something else. Then I felt the same way anyone can
feel in high altitude: I was numbed but when flying, I swallow
and it goes away. But in this case the numbness remained for
days on end and then the noise started progressively from
occasional drops, until full scale city centre noise.

---

24. Email: R_Not_REPLIED

ROOSEVELT When I first realised I had T, I started
remembering and I remembered that I could hear noises
before even as a kid.

I always assumed that my numbness was due to my sinuses or as a result of a bad cold so I took it for granted that it couldn't have been something else.

In recent years I became more conscious of it and before I just ignored it but it wasn't as strong and loud as it is now.

But when it became out of control, I knew I had it and we met and you told me I had T.

25. Email: R_Not_REPLIED

ROOSEVELT I have to get on with it. Isn't what you kept on saying to me? That's the only thing you ever told me.

Maybe you're right. Maybe that's the only thing that can be done. I can't live but I can survive. I wouldn't say I have to work since my family has provided me well enough to survive anyway.

ROOSEVELT I'm a politician. I want to be a great politician for the greater good. For people. My ambition is to become a senator. A republican senator. I can't be one if I listen to T. T will not control me. T will never control me. I want to marry my girlfriend and have kids. My girlfriend doesn't know I have T. She will never know: I have to hide it.

I need to. Who would want to marry anyone hearing voices? It's the first sign of madness.

27. Email: R_Not_REPLIED

ROOSEVELT

I must get on with it. I must ignore it.

I must get on with it. I must ignore it.

I must get on with it. I must ignore it.

I must get on with it. I must ignore it.

I must get on with it. I must ignore it.

I must get on with it. I must ignore it.

28. Email: R_Not_REPLIED

ROOSEVELT

I must get on with it. I must ignore it.

I must get on with it. I must ignore it.

I must get on with it. I must ignore it.

I must get on with it. I must ignore it.

I must get on with it. I must ignore it.

I must get on with it. I must ignore it.

29. Email: R_Not_REPLIED

ROOSEVELT

I must get on with it. I must ignore it.

I must get on with it. I must ignore it.

I must get on with it. I must ignore it.

I must get on with it. I must ignore it.

I must get on with it. I must ignore it.

I must get on with it. I must ignore it.

30. Email: R_Not_REPLIED

ROOSEVELT

I must get on with it. I must ignore it.

I must get on with it. I must ignore it.

I must get on with it. I must ignore it.

I must get on with it. I must ignore it.

I must get on with it. I must ignore it.

I must get on with it. I must ignore it.

---

31. Email: R_Not_REPLIED

ROOSEVELT

I must get on with it. I must ignore it.

I must get on with it. I must ignore it.

I must get on with it. I must ignore it.

I must get on with it. I must ignore it.

I must get on with it. I must ignore it.

I must get on with it. I must ignore it.

32. Email: R_Not_REPLIED

ROOSEVELT

I must get on with it. I must ignore it.

I must get on with it. I must ignore it.

I must get on with it. I must ignore it.

I must get on with it. I must ignore it.

I must get on with it. I must ignore it.

I must get on with it. I must ignore it.

33. Email: R_Not_REPLIED

ROOSEVELT T is trying to say something to me but I can't understand it and never will. I will never let T control me: I will never listen to T. Never. If I do, I'll die.

34. Email: R_Not_REPLIED

ROOSEVELT I will not let T kill me. If I die it is because my subconscious wants it. If I live it's the ultimate natural self-defence from my brain: the only protection my brain has against T: sudden death.

ROOSEVELT I want to live so it's up to me to ignore and fight T before my brain kills T and myself in the process.

36. Email: R_Not_REPLIED

ROOSEVELT

T will never kill me.

T will never kill me.

T will never kill me.

T will never kill me.

T will never kill me.

T will never kill me.

37. Email: R_Not_REPLIED

ROOSEVELT I can't kill T either and I can't let my brain kill T. I must get on with it. I must ignore it.

38. Email: R_Not_REPLIED

ROOSEVELT

I must get on with it. I must ignore it.

I must get on with it. I must ignore it.

I must get on with it. I must ignore it.

I must get on with it. I must ignore it.

I must get on with it. I must ignore it.

I must get on with it. I must ignore it.

---

39. Email: R_Not_REPLIED

ROOSEVELT

I must get on with it. I must ignore it.

I must get on with it. I must ignore it.

I must get on with it. I must ignore it.

I must get on with it. I must ignore it.

I must get on with it. I must ignore it.

I must get on with it. I must ignore it.

40. Email: R_Not_REPLIED

ROOSEVELT

I must get on with it. I must ignore it.

I must get on with it. I must ignore it.

I must get on with it. I must ignore it.

I must get on with it. I must ignore it.

I must get on with it. I must ignore it.

I must get on with it. I must ignore it.

41. Email: R_Not_REPLIED

ROOSEVELT

I must get on with it. I must ignore it.

I must get on with it. I must ignore it.

I must get on with it. I must ignore it.

I must get on with it. I must ignore it.

I must get on with it. I must ignore it.

I must get on with it. I must ignore it.

42. Email: R_Not_REPLIED

ROOSEVELT

I must get on with it. I must ignore it.

I must get on with it. I must ignore it.

I must get on with it. I must ignore it.

I must get on with it. I must ignore it.

I must get on with it. I must ignore it.

I must get on with it. I must ignore it.

43. Email: R_Not_REPLIED

ROOSEVELT

I must get on with it. I must ignore it.

I must get on with it. I must ignore it.

I must get on with it. I must ignore it.

I must get on with it. I must ignore it.

I must get on with it. I must ignore it.

I must get on with it. I must ignore it.

ROOSEVELT I will go through with it. I will be a senator. I'll prove it to you! See you in six years' time.

Six is my number. I don't know why. It has always been like this. Whatever I do in life, whatever I do the number 6 always crops up.

45. Email: R_Not_REPLIED

ROOSEVELT Where are you, DOC? WHERE ARE YOU?

46. Email: R_Not_REPLIED

ROOSEVELT I have called the centre a few times and they are getting really worried. Where are you?

47. Email: R_Not_REPLIED

ROOSEVELT Whenever I call the centre I can never remember your name. They know you because they know that

I'm your patient.

I remember everything but I can't remember your name. I just call you DOC. Why can't I remember your name?

You do exist, don't you? We have met. You do exist, you must be real.

48. Email: R_Not_REPLIED

ROOSEVELT My head is like the whole engine of a fast train working at full speed and there is still no sign of you.

49. Email: R_Not_REPLIED

ROOSEVELT I have called the centre and they don't know where you are. Where are you?

50. Email: R_Not_REPLIED

ROOSEVELT DOC: I've called the centre again. What happened? Tell me it's not true! You do exist, don't you? Reply to me, please. YOU HAVE TO!

---

51. Email: R_Not_REPLIED

ROOSEVELT Where are you DOC? Is this true? Really true?
They've told me you're dead. Shot dead. I don't believe it. I
know you're still alive somewhere. Tell me!

---

52. Email: R_Not_REPLIED

ROOSEVELT DOC: I went to the police and asked them. They
told me you're dead. DEAD! Someone slit your throat then
shot you in the face, in your eyes then in your heart. DOC. I'm
sure you can read these lines even if you're dead. DOC. I know
you can DOC. You have a new life somewhere but you can still
read my emails.

---

53. Email: R_Not_REPLIED

ROOSEVELT

WHERE ARE YOU DOC?

WHERE ARE YOU DOC?

WHERE ARE YOU DOC?

WHERE ARE YOU DOC?

WHERE ARE YOU DOC?

WHERE ARE YOU DOC?

54. Email: R_Not_REPLIED

ROOSEVELT

WHERE ARE YOU DOC?

WHERE ARE YOU DOC?

WHERE ARE YOU DOC?

WHERE ARE YOU DOC?

WHERE ARE YOU DOC?

WHERE ARE YOU DOC?

55. Email: R_Not_REPLIED

ROOSEVELT

WHERE ARE YOU DOC?

WHERE ARE YOU DOC?

WHERE ARE YOU DOC?

WHERE ARE YOU DOC?

WHERE ARE YOU DOC?

WHERE ARE YOU DOC?

56. Email: R_Not_REPLIED

ROOSEVELT

WHERE ARE YOU DOC?

WHERE ARE YOU DOC?

WHERE ARE YOU DOC?

WHERE ARE YOU DOC?

WHERE ARE YOU DOC?

WHERE ARE YOU DOC?

57. Email: R_Not_REPLIED

ROOSEVELT

WHERE ARE YOU DOC?

WHERE ARE YOU DOC?

WHERE ARE YOU DOC?

WHERE ARE YOU DOC?

WHERE ARE YOU DOC?

WHERE ARE YOU DOC?

58. Email: R_Not_REPLIED

ROOSEVELT

WHERE ARE YOU DOC?

WHERE ARE YOU DOC?

WHERE ARE YOU DOC?

WHERE ARE YOU DOC?

WHERE ARE YOU DOC?

WHERE ARE YOU DOC?

59. Email: R_Not_REPLIED

ROOSEVELT

WHERE ARE YOU DOC?

WHERE ARE YOU DOC?

WHERE ARE YOU DOC?

WHERE ARE YOU DOC?

WHERE ARE YOU DOC?

WHERE ARE YOU DOC?

---

60. Email: R_Not_REPLIED

ROOSEVELT

WHERE ARE YOU DOC?

WHERE ARE YOU DOC?

WHERE ARE YOU DOC?

WHERE ARE YOU DOC?

WHERE ARE YOU DOC?

WHERE ARE YOU DOC?

61. Email: R_Not_REPLIED

ROOSEVELT

WHERE ARE YOU DOC?

WHERE ARE YOU DOC?

WHERE ARE YOU DOC?

WHERE ARE YOU DOC?

WHERE ARE YOU DOC?

WHERE ARE YOU DOC?

62. Email: R_Not_REPLIED

ROOSEVELT

WHERE ARE YOU DOC?

WHERE ARE YOU DOC?

WHERE ARE YOU DOC?

WHERE ARE YOU DOC?

WHERE ARE YOU DOC?

WHERE ARE YOU DOC?

63. Email: R_Not_REPLIED

ROOSEVELT

WHERE ARE YOU DOC?

WHERE ARE YOU DOC?

WHERE ARE YOU DOC?

WHERE ARE YOU DOC?

WHERE ARE YOU DOC?

WHERE ARE YOU DOC?

---

64. Email: R_Not_REPLIED

ROOSEVELT

WHERE ARE YOU DOC?

WHERE ARE YOU DOC?

WHERE ARE YOU DOC?

WHERE ARE YOU DOC?

WHERE ARE YOU DOC?

WHERE ARE YOU DOC?

65. Email: R_Not_REPLIED

ROOSEVELT

WHERE ARE YOU DOC?

WHERE ARE YOU DOC?

WHERE ARE YOU DOC?

WHERE ARE YOU DOC?

WHERE ARE YOU DOC?

66. Email: R_Not_REPLIED

ROOSEVELT DOC! I had this sinking feeling that you're no longer there. That you're... dead. You're no longer there, are you DOC? That's why you couldn't reply to my emails. Somehow you have been a big part of my life even for a short moment in time. Good bye, DOC!

<u>Mail failure, return to sender</u>

----- Original message -----

X--DKIM-Signature: v=1; a=rsa-sh; c=relaxed/relaxed;

   d=dickhead.com; s=20120113;

   h=mime-version:sender:x-originating-ip:date:x-dick-sender-auth

   :message-id:subject:from:to:content-type:x-gm-message-state;

   bh=DFxcm5SqgeuEg71554tTl/04qGk1VFg=;

b=SkTaRFIwl6xJaI6DkGr7dMYMu2koeRn1lxmOWMUZEzJA
T6nid4QcOWwM0HJKaSzhDZ

InJ2MAix8/7sg65qkVLeIjCAkBuen0Rpm10FkZK/+Dng9V4A/7
h7ue3Kib2j

9+RrlPpknL1E+Bszc45dy+mulxh1m0iwCDf2Z1zTV5CBtHxLH

4NGmA0GkheL68XLfU3Te2xVabFEeIN0INdX0Nyp09pkOoyR
H

jS4Iz6lq37r36xpysgPrpgWBZkzpuL3WT1tFpz3mKdpJ9F

URxA==

MIME-Version: 1.0

Received: by 10.204.148.72 with SMTP id
o8mr2926180bkv.127.1339777066763; Fri,

 15 Jun 2012 09:17:46 -0700 (PDT)

Sender: Roosevelt

Received: by 10.205.26.6 with HTTP; Fri, 15 Jun 2012 09:17:44 -
0700 (PDT)

X-Originating-IP: [657]

Date: Fri, 15 Jun 2012 17:17:44 +0100

X--Sender-Auth: xgH6ppKeWGQeZ7krxM

Message-ID: <f07uwqJCeXSv_jg@dick.com>

Subject: Follow up Treatment

From: Roosevelt <r@r>

To: DOC@DOC

Content-Type: multipart/mixed;
boundary=0015175cab32248a6d04c285287c

X-Gm-Message-State:
ALoCoQnVt1nBTE8BCDdkh2hjr44uqOD9xJSl

<u>Act 3:</u> LIVE

1. TV NEWS   Introducing the action where and when G meets Mr Roosevelt, now the current president of the United States live on TV.
2. HOSTAGE   G has taken the president hostage.
3. OUTRO: G meets his destiny
4. Previously, at the CENTER

DOC's final report five years ago

LIVE TV NEWS

TV 1   1. We interrupt our program to report that our President Roosevelt the Second has just been held at gunpoint by what appears to be a lunatic, hysterical man in his twenties or even younger.

TV 2   2. What is actually happening?

TV 1   3. What we are witnessing here is the sheer horror of seeing our beloved president at the mercy of a lone and desperate gunman.

TV 2   4. The president is still being held at gunpoint. They are slowly running towards the left of the building followed from a fair distance by all possible police forces and Federal agents.

TV 1   5. The gunman is shouting repeatedly at the president's entourage to back off and the president seems to have echoed this order.

TV 2   6. The president is held firmly by the still unknown man.

TV 1   7. The president and the gunman are now moving backwards. The gun man appears to be in a very desperate state and is screaming at the Federal agents but we do not have any audio as yet. The president seems to indicate to everyone to back off.

TV 2   8. They are now moving backwards again. I just got a message saying that they are at a standstill. No one is moving...
#Short Pause

It is now complete silence on the 66th floor of the new Tower building; a new building of 66 floors that has just been inaugurated by the president.

TV 1   9. We can hear them again: yes, they are moving again, they are turning through a staircase. Shots can be heard; the FBI agents just fired... They, they... What's going on? Where are they? The FBI agents are moving in all directions. Where are they? Any footage?

TV 2   We have just heard a very loud explosion…

TV 1   That's right; it seems to have been triggered when the FBI agents opened fire.

TV 2   We have just lost them!

TV 1   What? Where?

TV 2   We can confirm that the president has just disappeared; they seem to have fallen inside a ventilation system. Every effort is now underway to dismantle the ventilation system.

TV 1   Meanwhile on the ground outside the building a huge crowd of hundreds of people is standing outside the new Tower building.

TV 2   10. If you've just tuned in, the President of the United States, President Roosevelt the Second on an inaugural visit to the new Tower building of 66 floors from West Virginia Street has been held at gunpoint then abducted. After a short exchange with the FBI agents, the president and the gunman have vanished inside a ventilation system.

TV 1   That's right Tracy, vanished. It's live and it's...astounding!

TV 2   Do we have any details now?

TV 1   Oh, but yes, they have been tracked down...They are...Where? Inside an elevator or another room, it is unclear but the door seems to be blocked.

TV 2   How do you mean "blocked"?

TV 1   Malfunctioning, as it seems...

TV 2   Are they inside the elevator or are they not?

TV 1   They seem to be inside a room but it is stuck. They can't open the doors. This is mind-blowing stuff, Tracy!

TV 2   Indeed, it is!

#Footage of the president's capture seen from different angles is played and re-played in the background

11.

TV 1   Still no news of President Roosevelt the Second and his gun man and we still don't know who this guy is.

TV 2   Any news about where the President's wife is? Does she know?

TV 1   No details on this either, I dread to think!

TV 2   Oh my God, what is happening now? Where are they?

TV 1   They may be dead...

TV 2   They may be dead now!

LIVE HOSTAGE

#3-1a. The gunman and the president are slowly moving along on the floor followed by the President's entourage.

Without warning and suddenly the FBI men open fire... Shooting indiscriminately in front of them...

3-3. A loud banging noise is heard and both the gunman and the President run to take cover inside a room. The FBI men are following them and fire again. A small part of the wall in front of them collapses into pieces and parts of the ceiling disintegrate. A big white cloud of dust has recovered the room, the situation is extremely confused. The FBI men are shouting repeatedly the same phrases: "Where are they?" "What's going on?" "What now?"

The gun man and the President have now disappeared from sight.

3-1c. Meanwhile the gunman and the President have taken refuge inside a bathroom. The gunman locks the door from the inside. All of a sudden, a loud bang followed by what seems like an explosion is heard. The FBI agents are desperately trying to unlock the door then open the door but it's stuck. There are no windows; the president and the gunman are trapped inside the bathroom.

3-2a. They both glance around the room for a minute.

3-2b.

ROOSEVELT We're stuck now!

G We can't be…

ROOSEVELT *He starts screaming* Help, we're here!

G Hey, shut the fuck up! I've got a gun here!

ROOSEVELT And what use will it do?

G What fucking use?

ROOSEVELT Go ahead, kill me! Then you might kill yourself soon after!

G Fuck you! I've got a gun here!

ROOSEVELT It's America, pal! Everyone's got a gun.

G Who's fucking everyone?

ROOSEVELT I've got one too

#The President fetches his gun from underneath his shirt

G Fuck you! Now we both have guns!

ROOSEVELT What can we do with two guns?

G I'm the one holding you prisoner here!

ROOSEVELT We're both prisoners now!

G Fuck you!

ROOSEVELT Yep!

3-3a. *#They each have a gun pointed at the other's head*

G What now?

ROOSEVELT I don't know...

G We can't fucking stay here forever!

ROOSEVELT They'll find us but we may be trapped for a while

#They are both circling around together in the middle of the bathroom still pointing the guns at each other

3-4a

ROOSEVELT What's your name?

G What?

ROOSEVELT What's your name?

G G-Gordon

ROOSEVELT Pleased to meet you G!

G *#Slightly frightened and bewildered*

ROOSEVELT My name is President Roosevelt the Second, President of the United States of America

G I know!

ROOSEVELT You're pointing a gun at the president of the United States of America?

#At this point, they are both withdrawing their weapons.

They both stare at the room for 66 seconds and they are still holding their guns. Various noises can be heard almost like in a symphony and by the 66th second some incoherent voices can be heard.

G I guess we don't need guns anymore

ROOSEVELT I guess not…

#They are both dropping their guns at the same time inside a big trash near the main sink

3-5a.

#G keeps on shaking his head and with one finger from each hand is trying to clean his ears

ROOSEVELT What's up with your head?

G It's fucking inside: the noise, the engine, "them" and that noise...

ROOSEVELT You...

G It is constant now; it was sporadic but not anymore.

ROOSEVELT You have Tinnitus...

G Yeah, man. Fucking Tinnitus!

ROOSEVELT *#The president stares at G in amazement...*

G Fucking because of people like you and the life we have to lead.

ROOSEVELT Not people like me; I'm the same...

G What fucking same?

ROOSEVELT I have Tinnitus

G You?

ROOSEVELT For about twenty years, I probably always had "it". But when I was a kid, it was different then…

G You've got T...

ROOSEVELT Yeah. All the time...

G You don't show "it"...

ROOSEVELT I do... in private. I've got to live with "it", I'm the president!

G Fuck!

ROOSEVELT Yes and no one will understand this...

G The ghosts...

ROOSEVELT The ghosts inside the machine...

G …and we've got them!

#G and President Roosevelt the Second in unison

ROOSEVELT G Because: "we have to live with it"!

#They both hold a deep breath and stare at each other for 66 seconds

G It's piercing loud…

ROOSEVELT Yes

G Thick…

ROOSEVELT Yeah

G It is breaking glasses…

ROOSEVELT I know

G They're telling me something

ROOSEVELT I know

G They wanted me to do this…

ROOSEVELT I know…

G I'm so fucked up…

ROOSEVELT Don't listen to "it"!

G I have to…

ROOSEVELT Ignore "it"!

G The ghosts…

ROOSEVELT Leave "them" out!

3-6a.

G No...

#G falls on the floor and agonises; rolling over the floor, holding his head with his hands

ROOSEVELT I can't let go. I can't let myself down. If I do, there is no control; there is no stopping me. I can't be next to someone like you...

3-7a.

#They are now both covering their ears with their hands. The President stands for a few seconds then collapses on the floor and rolls over the floor along with G for 66 seconds. After a few seconds the sound of what is going on in their heads echoes in the bathroom for another 66 seconds

#They are now both lying down on the floor

ROOSEVELT Do you remember things?

G Yes, everything

ROOSEVELT I mean when you were a kid?

G Yes. I remember everything since I was born, man! It's all there, all the noise...The shit I got from the cops, the food I stole when I got five, when my dad used to punch me when I was ten.

ROOSEVELT Do you spend time remembering?

G Yeah, all the time; every day and every hour… That's how I get through all the stuff. I remember the first noise my first gun made when I fired in the air...

ROOSEVELT Do you remember the taste of things?

G Yeah, man. I remember everything.

ROOSEVELT They say that you can't clear the present without remembering the past and without a "cleared" present, we can't get a future.

G I'm not sure I get this. The noise is moving now: water is flowing.

ROOSEVELT Do you remember the voices who told you to hold me up? Have the voices told you to kill me?

G No, I don't think so. There are just too many voices. It could take forever to list them!

ROOSEVELT I know. I started to do this many years ago.

G Does anyone know of you?

ROOSEVELT No one except there was a shrink I've told a long time ago.

G Kids?

ROOSEVELT Yes, you didn't know?

G I only know you're the president because I was around and there was this crowd around you.

ROOSEVELT Didn't you vote?

G Fuck no! I didn't even know who you were!

ROOSEVELT Well, I've got three kids, three boys...

G ...All with T?

ROOSEVELT No, but it may come later.

G I feel better now!

ROOSEVELT I'm glad. You have kids?

G Me? Fuck no! I had a few girls... Don't know anyone, nobody knows me, I'm a "no-body" and no one knows I've got T. except...There was a doc, a long time ago.

ROOSEVELT Was it a spur of the moment this hold-up?

G Yes! I was there and you were there. I had enough of it and it was you or I had to jump over...

ROOSEVELT Jump from the 66th floor?

G Yeah, man!

ROOSEVELT I'm glad you made it here…

G …Yeah but for how long?

ROOSEVELT I can't answer that!

G You're FBI security people are useless!

ROOSEVELT I know!

G Knowing things doesn't help. There are things that we know, but knowing them can get you killed!

ROOSEVELT We know things that we're not supposed to know, but we know them anyway. The things that we know are memorised and computed for T. T gets to know the things that we know and T controls them. T will use the stuff that we know. We can't let T get hold of the things that we know.

G I know! I keep on fighting the ghosts in the machine and the war is so deafening...

3-9a.

G ROOSEVELT   *#They are now both sitting on the floor, in the middle of the bathroom back to back*

G I did this because I had to.

ROOSEVELT You didn't have to do anything.

G I had to do it because I needed to do it.

ROOSEVELT You didn't need to do it.

G We have to do things, we're controlled.

ROOSEVELT We don't have to do anything; break the control.

G I can't break this control, it has already overpowered me.

ROOSEVELT I break it every day; the voices are constantly trying to control me.

G You're the president's guy; you people always try to control people.

ROOSEVELT We never control anyone, we let people control themselves.

G You people are forcing people like me to be controlled!

ROOSEVELT We're not forcing anyone; we guide in order to save you from being controlled.

G Who needs to be guided by you people? They say there are six people ruling the world and you're doing their dirty work for them.

ROOSEVELT There are more than six groups of people ruling the world and we're merely the in-between filter.

G A filter with leaks: we get harassed all the time...

ROOSEVELT Ignore people, learn to love them.

G I can't ignore people, I hate them.

ROOSEVELT Don't hate anyone!

G I do hate everyone.

ROOSEVELT You're not that fucked up

G I'm completely fucked up, man!

ROOSEVELT Ignore the noise, fight the ghosts!

G I can't ignore the noise, the ghosts have overpowered me.

ROOSEVELT Think of different things; move away and concentrate!

G I can't think of different things, I can't move.

ROOSEVELT I can't help you, you're a prisoner!

G Why would you help me? I've kidnapped you!

ROOSEVELT Prisoners can escape!

G Not from a high-security jail that you people created!

ROOSEVELT You can try!

G You people made it too impossible!

ROOSEVELT Escape!

G I have tried man! I nearly died!

ROOSEVELT Don't kill yourself!

G I have many times, it never worked!

ROOSEVELT You need your brain plugged!

G Maybe I do and maybe I don't...

ROOSEVELT I'll get my head plugged if you get yours
plugged!

G If you pay for it, I'll do it!

ROOSEVELT Surgery may not work...

G We can try...

ROOSEVELT G *#They both get up and scream in unison* This
is hell!

G So much so for the psycho-class, doc!

ROOSEVELT Anytime, G!

3-10a.

*#Both are staring at one another in the eyes continuously for
sixty-six seconds. The noises are getting progressively louder
and the voices clearer, from previous conversations they had in
the past until their own distorted voices can be heard in the
background giving them orders.*

3-11a.

ROOSEVELT G

#Both explode in some hysterical laughter for sixty-six seconds.

Almost in unison G and President Roosevelt the Second.

Oh, God it hurts!

LIVE   THE RESCUE

4-1a.

TV NEWS

#The presenters describe the rescue mission and the footage of the action is projected in the background.

TV 1   The rescue team has finally entered the floor where the doors have been stuck. Every effort is made to break the doors.

TV 2   6 crash shooters are being deployed into position... And still nothing is moving...

TV 1   This silence is deafening...

#Short pause

TV 2   The visual is on but no audio.

TV 1   What is happening? The doors open very slowly... The president is standing on the left and the gunman is on the right. The gun man doesn't seem to be pointing at the president anymore; indeed, he doesn't seem to hold his gun anymore.

TV 2   We have the audio now: we can hear the president screaming...

ROOSEVELT   Don't shoot!

4-2a.

G ROOSEVELT   *#The scene occurs in slow motion*

TV 1   The gunman falls slowly on the floor, perforated by gun fire; his blood is dripping from all over and gushing into the air...

#He is now dead on the floor with his eyes wide open.

TV 2   The president kneels over the body and closes the eyes of the unknown gunman.

TV 1   It's an atrocious sight! It's the end.

LIVE OUTRO

Previously, at the CENTER

*#Extract from DOC's concluding statement N.666 on the T
condition suffered by G and Mr Roosevelt*

Tinnitus is a human condition (although it almost certainly
applies to other members of the animal kingdom) triggering
heavy and incoherent noises to be heard and this sensation
makes it feel as if the noise is coming or has been generated from
inside the brain.

This noise can be sporadic or constant, little or as heavy as the
engine of a plane or some broken pieces of glass in a loop.

Often when the noise is too loud, there is a sentiment of voices
being heard.

It is not a curable condition and it is evolving. Anyone can either
be born with it or it could have been gradually developed
mainly due to some extreme stress, extreme noises (such as
unregulated piercing police and ambulance cars' sirens, heavy

music or a prolonged contact with a cell phone too close to the head).

A large amount of the human population has one form or another of Tinnitus but most wouldn't realise it until it becomes serious; the noise becomes omnipresent and causes hearing impairment. The seriousness of the condition can grow only by allowing it to develop by encouraging a stressful lifestyle, lack of exercise, hearing loud noises, watching TV for too long or drinking black tea or coffee. It has been established by many scientists that a time bomb is ticking since it could literally affect anyone.

The catchphrase provided by most doctors is: "just get on with it, ignore it and change your lifestyle". Not a long-term solution for a time bomb waiting to explode. It is not regarded as a disease or even a mental condition or an illness and yet this condition can easily paralyse the brain if not taken under control. Many people became addicted to painkillers and sleeping tablets as a result. It is not uncommon to witness people rolling on the floor in agony as the noise becomes deafening and insufferable. In this case many doctors might suspect drug abuse or some mental illness.

We are a machine and if we are invaded and controlled by some unknown forces; noises, ghosts or otherwise the consequences can be devastating for the sufferer but also for anyone else in close contact.

5. G's Forbidden Thoughts

The Forbidden **Thoughts** are the abusing language hurled at G's receiver's end during some close encounters.

The **thoughts** have not been displayed during the course of the action as they would have been in the way of the story and would have given away the plot during the process of the interviews.

1. Interview 49

She was patronising, obnoxious and pretentious. She deserved to die. She "knew it all". She would not listen to anyone or anything. She would go on ignoring people. You can't ignore people: you may not like someone but can't ignore anything. Especially when you're paid to do so.

She was so terrified, she was frozen stiff, unable to respond: there was a knife held to the left side of her brain and an excruciating order conveyed in a rational, whispered and serene manner to swallow a small kitchen knife. Easy. She died a few hours later, half strangled by the knife and half exhausted by the fear and sheer horror of the act.

2. Interview 50

Her throat was slit open and it bled like there is no tomorrow. It was such a splendid show! Shame you missed it. She struggled for her breath for a good 66 minutes. A perfect death: genius!

3. Interview 51

Such a pussy boy. You never lived and will never live long enough to really live and you still believe that you "know it all".

4. Interview 52

I will be fucking breaking every fucking bone in your body leaving you crawling on the streets for the rest of your fucking brain-dead life.

5. Interview 55

T will kill you one day and you will be desiccated like a rat in a lab. You're a scientist, you're destined to be slaughtered. You need to know what it's like, why and how you are being sacrificed for the greater good. Funny how it ends up being what body parts can fit down the toilet or in the freezer -if you're rich enough to own one that is. And the answer is not many.

6. Interview 57

He was too big for his own good. Too fat. Why are people like that running the show and always so unhealthy? And the medical staff! And telling me that I should eat more. Who wants to end up like them? You should have seen how he stuffed his face. He didn't even notice that a fork had been inserted inside his cake. He choked, almost in his own vomit. Too easy! He'll never know why he needed to die. A major regret there.

The END

Long Summary

An interactive novel, murder, mystery thriller in 3 acts revolving around the number 6 and the letter T, both being the proton and neutron of the story. Two men from very different backgrounds meet and discover that they are both guided by invisible ghosts and they are in fact two machines forced to live a life haunted by an incurable condition.

During the inauguration of the tallest building in town, one man is holding the President of the United States at gunpoint and together they will disappear for 66 minutes out of the eyes of the world where they will confront the ghosts in the machine. T.

The story is presented in four distinctive chapters: Chapter 1. The main characters are being introduced to the reader by their psychiatrist inside a medical centre. The two main protagonists G and Roosevelt never actually meet, although their paths crossed once at the centre but they both have been oblivious of this encounter. The story and description of "T" and the ghost or ghosts (plural: T being multiplied in the machine but always remaining under the umbrella and the main "T" monster). There is a gradual introduction on how T progresses within G's and Roosevelt's heads. During the course of the first chapter the reader will witness a series of murders being committed at the centre foreboding the way the main story is shaping. G and Roosevelt have both ended their sojourn at the medical centre. They have been offered a follow-up treatment by their psychiatrist by email.

In chapter two the reader is getting acquainted with the private life and history of the main protagonists. A graphic evolution of T's life and existence is revealed and a slow build-up to elucidate the murders that have occurred at the centre is taking place. The email exchange ends abruptly: G's and Roosevelt's emails are no longer replied to. Something has happened. Both protagonists continue to email DOC in the vain hope of an answer until DOC's mailbox is full to capacity and the emails are being returned.

During the series of "solo emails (or emails sent but not responded)" the murders committed at the centre in chapter 1 are slowly making sense and all the protagonists slowly evolve and transit towards their destiny.

The two main protagonists G and Roosevelt finally meet on the 66th floor of a new big tower being inaugurated. Roosevelt has achieved his ambitions: he mastered T and became President Roosevelt the Second president of the United States. G and President Roosevelt meet: G is taking the president hostage at gunpoint during a stand-off. Due to the incompetence of the FBI agents, when trying to free the president, an explosion occurred and they both disappeared, trapped inside a room. Together they will live 66 hours at the mercy of T until they are fully delivered by the FBI agents and G will meet his final destiny as described in chapter 1.

The murders are all implied in the story. They occur as we move on into the story. We can only picture and visualise one death in the story. The other murders occur as we move on into the story. We can only picture one death but in the story, it is not a murder but a legal shoot-out by the FBI. In real terms it was a murder that had been announced at the beginning of the story. The same character committed all the murders including triggering his own death, subconsciously or consciously in order to kill T, triggering the demon within him.

In a sense T is autobiographical as the author has been plagued
with the T condition ever since he can remember. As with most
of his stories and characters they are the sums of his close
encounters, chance meetings that drove him to meddle with a
diverse crowd in extremely surreal circumstances. It's all to do
with clear and concise observation: a daily practice and an ever-
over-serviced memory.

In Act II: Emails / 3- G Not Replied: it is not evident if G really
knows who killed Doc. Many killers do not realise that death is
final and they often kill in the vain hope that their victim should
only suffer whatever they believe they deserve but the next day
is another day and the killer may not feel the same way after that
and certainly not consciously realise what he/she may or may
have done.

Epilogue

How do we change things? Who is responsible?

It's never their fault. It is not my fault that you failed or anyone else's. Is this an act of God, in this case God and we need to put up with it or be anyone's fault - you or my fault as well as it happened to you and you either triggered it or had the problem in the first place? Anyone and everyone must work together to resolve the issue. no arrogance and no black mail-. God has lived on this Earth long enough to know that he is not political: neither left nor right.

Not to favour one newspaper or another but it happens to be this newspaper -who in the late 2010 years, asked the question: "Are we run by an evil sect?" The answer would be extremely inspirational but we mustn't forget that we can also be our own devil and the human race -and the rest of the animal kingdom- is always threatened by the others and the unknown and the primal instinct of survival is evil.
Everyone has got its own history and created his / her / its own history, recreating history from a different angle.

The world would be far better off without religion or if people could keep their religion to themselves. Just like politics. Politics and Religions have got nothing to do with government and the rule of law. One is one personal fantasy and the other is a method of ruling our existence that must only be run by professionals with no power whatsoever, all being state employees. Religion and politics invented evil. There are 5 devils: Baphomet, Beelzebub, Lucifer, Satan and Old Nick -yours truly, a registered name and no one can take it, thank you very much-. The King of all devils is Baphomet with the breasts of a woman but still a man, trust me, as I have met him. It's extraordinary that all the names of the devils are male. Evil comes in all shapes and sizes. Gender equality still has a long way to go. The bible is actually fascinating. My favourite bit remains The Mark of the Beast...

'And the second beast required all people small and great, rich and poor, free and slave, to receive a mark on their right hand or on their forehead, so that no one could buy or sell unless he had the mark— the name of the beast or the number of its name. Here is a call for wisdom: Let the one who has insight calculate the number of the beast, for it is the number of a man, and that number is 666.

These people who violate and kill others are monsters and yet they exist, they are in the bible and
the greatest problem of all is that anyone could potentially become a monster and our society
has not been prepared for this. There is no helpline where to go for help since any act of brutality will be dealt with by the police and not a good Samaritan.

There are absolutely no warning signs and no proactive system to prevent the unmentionable.

Stories abound in the news that for decades children in care homes have been brutally abused and yet very little is done to support them, if any support at all and barely any arrest and even if the monsters are arrested, there is no treatment.

Extreme violence can be triggered by all sorts of factors. Even though I was considered very cool and very calm and conciliant, I left one of my banks of 20 years after a string of fraudulent debits worth over £7000. I have been left stranded, empty-handed. I must have spent between 60 minutes and 120 minutes each time to complain over the phone, in various call centres located anywhere from China, India and even war-torn countries one can easily lose the plot. Some people got completely debilitated and walked into a branch only to be rebuffed by the staff who "only works there" and cannot help and found many violent interactions and fights inside various branches on YouTube videos. We have arrived in an age of being debilitated to the point of committing the unmentionable.

I have recently read in a newspaper that a chain of burgers used no less than 20 illegal ingredients in the food, to make it more enticing but at the same time the long-term side effects are extremely scary: mood swings, violent outbursts, depressions and daily angry exchanges with anyone in the vicinity of the protagonist.

Again, I'm not trying to excuse anything but just to raise the fact our society as it has become is clearly responsible. This is in no way trying to diminish the responsibility of any violent thugs or monsters or perhaps yes. If so, we need to criminalise our society; its managers and organisers.

I rest my case.

www.ingramcontent.com/pod-product-compliance
Lightning Source LLC
Chambersburg PA
CBHW060233100726
47907CB00003B/608